GRIDIRON GLORY

GRIDIRON GLORY

THE STORY OF THE
☆ ARMY-NAVY ☆
FOOTBALL RIVALRY

BARRY WILNER AND KEN RAPPOPORT

TAYLOR TRADE PUBLISHING

Lanham • New York • Boulder • Toronto • Oxford

*Dedicated to all the men and women who served in our Armed Forces
so that America could be free.*

Copyright © 2005 by Barry Wilner and Ken Rappoport
First Taylor Trade Publishing edition 2005

This Taylor Trade Publishing **hardback** edition of *Gridiron Glory* is an original
publication. It is published by arrangement with the author.

Published by Taylor Trade Publishing
An imprint of The Rowman & Littlefield Publishing Group, Inc.
4501 Forbes Boulevard, Suite 200, Lanham, Maryland 20706

Distributed by NATIONAL BOOK NETWORK

Library of Congress Cataloging-in-Publication Data

Wilner, Barry.
    Gridiron glory : the story of the Army-Navy football rivalry / Barry Wilner
and Ken Rappoport.— 1st Taylor Trade Publishing ed.
        p.   cm.
    ISBN 1-58979-277-7 (cloth : alk. paper)
    1. United States Military Academy—Football—History.   2. United States
Naval   Academy—Football—History.   3. Sports rivalries—United States.
I. Rappoport, Ken.   II. Title.
GV957.A7W55   2005
796.332'63—dc22   2005016248

⊗ ™ The paper used in this publication meets the minimum requirements of
American National Standard for Information Sciences—Permanence of Paper for
Printed Library Materials, ANSI/NISO Z39.48-1992.

Manufactured in the United States of America.

CONTENTS

ACKNOWLEDGMENTS

This book was a labor of love for both of us. We have combined on several other projects and, separately, have written dozens of books. None of them was as enlightening or rewarding in its research as this endeavor.

It was just plain fun to delve deeply into the best rivalry in sports.

But we also learned some valuable lessons about commitment and courage, about dedication and desire, about passion, pageantry, and patriotism. We hope our readers feel the same way.

We would like to thank the many people at both military academies for their assistance in compiling this book. Most notably, our deepest appreciation goes out to Ben Kotwica, Aaron Rigby, and Brian Drechsler—not only for their contributions to our project, but for their bravery and selflessness in protecting our families and our freedoms.

And a note of gratitude to Mike Albright, Carolyn Andros, Bob Beretta, Joel Blumberg, Mike Hogan, Bob Kinney, Rob Maaddi, Tony Roberts, Rick Roper, and Scott Strasemeier.

And, of course, to every Cadet and every Middie who ever suited up—on the football field and off it.

Ken Rappoport and Barry Wilner

INTRODUCTION

An excited, exhilarated sellout crowd jammed Baltimore's PSINet Stadium for a college football game. Millions more watched on television. Others, at distant corners of the world, listened to the broadcast of the game on radio.

A battle for the national championship? No. Not even close. These teams had an embarrassing combined record of 1-19, worst ever in their history.

There were no Heisman Trophy candidates in the bunch. Not even an NFL prospect.

And the game was played in numbing cold in December 2000, an excuse for anyone to stay home and watch it from the coziness of the living room. Yet 70,685 passionate fans braved the raw weather to root for their team.

Welcome to Army-Navy, the purest rivalry in college football and perhaps in all of team sports.

There are plenty of rivalries to keep spirits up during the college football season. Take your pick. There are cross-country (Notre Dame-Southern Cal), cross-town (UCLA-Southern Cal), regional (Harvard-Yale and Michigan-Ohio State), border (Oklahoma-Texas) and intrastate (Texas-Texas A&M), to name a few. Nor do small colleges take a back seat when it comes to the Big Game. Witness the most-played rivalry between Lafayette and Lehigh.

All great rivalries, for sure.

But the Army-Navy rivalry is different.

For instance, how many of the players in those other rivalries can say they think and talk about their greatest rival year round, 24/7?

Army and Navy do. It's part of the deal of attending the academies.

From the moment a freshman arrives at the Naval Academy, he is put on notice about the Army-Navy rivalry.

"The day you walk into the academy," says Roger Staubach, the great Navy quarterback of the 1960s, "they give you a haircut and then they say, 'Beat Army!'"

Staubach, who later became a star in the NFL and played in four Super Bowls with the Dallas Cowboys, was admittedly more nervous when he played in his first Army-Navy game.

Beat Army!

It is the most important expression a young sailor will ever voice in his four years at Annapolis.

And he says it every day when addressing an upperclassman. Or he scribbles it on a test paper if he wants to make any more points.

At West Point, it's the same story:

Beat Navy! Or Beat Navy, Sir! Or Beat the Hell out of Navy, Sir!

Try and beat that.

Other rivalries have pomp and pageantry.

The Army-Navy game has all that, and more.

The synchronized march of the Midshipmen and Cadets in perfect lockstep into the stadium before the game.

Fighter jets roaring over the stadium . . . gunship helicop-

Against a backdrop of Cadets, the Midshipmen march into the stadium.
Courtesy of the United States Naval Academy

ters making a sinister pass . . . parachutists floating to the turf of the football field. The show of force by the armed services is both awe-inspiring and ear-splitting.

It's more than that, though.

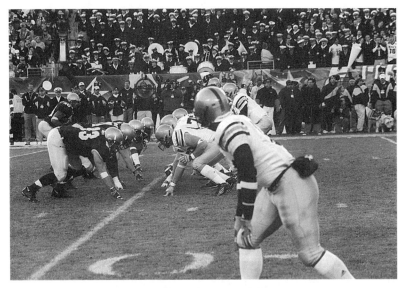

Army-Navy ready to charge in the 2004 game.
Photo by Ken Rappoport

"Some say it's the national television coverage and the 70,000 people in the stands that makes this game so big, but if you have ever been involved in it you know it isn't true," said Mark Pimpo, co-captain of the 1988 Navy team.

"I would feel the same and the game would mean as much if we played it in some back alley in South Philly. Everyone talks about the pageantry that is a great part of the game, but it's the competition that makes the Army-Navy game what it is."

Some players in other rivalries can start thinking about fighting for a job in the NFL when they graduate. Players in the Army-Navy game are thinking about fighting in Iraq and other distance places, and about their fallen buddies in the war.

For most of the seniors, the Army-Navy game is the last football game they'll play, good enough reason to go all out.

No other rivalry has a reason like that.

The world of the Cadets and Middies stops for one emotional day to focus on the traditional game that can make or break a season for either team. "One thing about the Army-Navy game you always remember is the two weeks of buildup," former Navy player and coach George Welsh said. "It's endless. It seems as if the game is never going to get here."

When it does, it commands widespread attention.

"Someone had a father, uncle, or brother in the Army or Navy," said Carl Ullrich, an athletic director at both Navy and Army. "Maybe the Marine man roots for the Navy, or maybe against him."

Say what you want about all the other rivalries, it's likely none are inflamed at the fever pitch of Army-Navy. It's not just a game. It's not just an event. It's an all-out war between athletes who will battle each other until the last man is standing, then stand side by side to fight for their country.

No other rivalry has a cause like that.

"We're brothers," said Gino Marchetti, who played noseguard for Navy in the 1990s. "You know in eight months, the guy across from you will be in a tank or commanding an infantry battalion. So you know he's not playing for the money or the stats."

There are usually no hard feelings between the teams, only hard hitting.

"Some good friendships were formed," Steve Belichick remembered of his association with the game as a longtime scout for Navy. "But come the Army-Navy weekend, it was 'buckle 'em up and let's go after each other, the fur is going to fly.'"

The game is always the last of the regular season for both teams. But they begin focusing on it long before the season starts. The "Beat Army!" and "Beat Navy!" chants continue right up to the day of the game when the Corps and the Brigade stage their traditional march into the stadium. Early in the morning, spit-and-polished Cadets in their military grays and Midshipmen in their blues board buses for the ride to the game.

Three hours before the start of the contest, they march in neat rows into the stadium, as if choreographed by a Hollywood director. Fans are already there to see the precision military marching show.

After that, forget about proper military conduct. The Cadets and Midshipmen might spend the afternoon shooting water balloons at each other. They stand and sway in unison throughout the game, cheering and singing like giddy college kids on a school break. Cannons blast after every score and at the end of each quarter, adding to the excitement of the moment. The postgame ritual is also something to see, and hear: players from both sides gather on the field and sing each

Navy coach Bill Elias (right) talks with John Cartwright (left) and the team captain Bob Wittenberg (middle) prior to the 1965 Army-Navy Football Classic.
Bettmann/CORBIS

school's alma mater in front of the other's cheering section, the winning school's song sung last.

Not even a war could diminish the power of this rivalry.

It was 1944. The first of the great wartime Army teams broke a five-year losing streak against Navy. General Douglas MacArthur, a fierce supporter of Army football, radioed from his headquarters in the South Pacific:

"The greatest of all Army teams. Stop. We have stopped the war to celebrate your magnificent success.

"MacArthur."

And for prisoners of war, the Army-Navy game was firmly in their thoughts in the most remote place—a camp near Hanoi during the Vietnam War.

The prisoners held a secret Army-Navy weekend. Tapping on the walls, they would communicate the progress of the imagined game until the ultimate conclusion. Then there were magnificent "menus" for postgame celebrations with lots of make-believe beer and pretzels. It helped the prisoners keep their sanity in horrendous conditions, according to naval commander Jack Fellows. These special "mind parties," plus pleasant recollections of past Army-Navy games, kept Fellows' psyche intact during his long, hard ordeal. He even made "bets" with Air Force men who were graduates of West Point.

Since the Army-Navy series started in 1890, there have been many memorable confrontations—not all of them on the field. The 1893 game, a 6-4 victory for Navy, sparked bloody battles in the stands and a heated exchange between a brigadier general and a rear admiral. Tempers rose higher and higher. Finally, the two challenged each other to a duel.

President Grover Cleveland was so enraged, he halted the series for five years.

The rivalry, interrupted briefly only three times since,

reached its 100th game in 1999 when Navy beat Army 19-9 and cut the Cadets' advantage in the series to 48-45-7.

Navy added another victory in 2000 to cut Army's lead to a mere two games after 101 played. And by 2004, following Navy's 42-13 victory, the teams were tied at 49-49-7. The series has been that close. And filled with plenty of surprises.

There were years when the presence of Army and Navy meant something in the national rankings.

In 1946, an unbeaten Army team featuring Glenn Davis ("Mr. Outside") and Doc Blanchard ("Mr. Inside") was headed for a third straight national championship. Navy had won only one game all season. Yet it looked as if the Midshipmen would pull off the biggest upset in the series. Trailing 21-18, they drove down the field, reaching the Army 2 when time ran out.

The close decision cost Army the national title, which went to Notre Dame that year.

In 1950, another powerful Army team coached by legendary Earl Blaik hoped to extend its overall winning streak to 29 when it met a weaker Navy team on the last day of the regular season. Army was 8-0 that year, Navy 2-8.

So, naturally, Navy knocked off Army 14-2. The upset established an era of naval supremacy that extended into the 1960s, when Navy's Heisman Trophy winning Staubach was the reigning star quarterback in college football.

The game that historians remember as the all-time classic was played in 1926 at snowy Soldier Field in Chicago. Navy was unbeaten that year and Army had lost only a 7-0 decision to Notre Dame.

The game ended in a 21-21 tie before 110,000 fans, then the largest crowd ever to see a college football game.

A spectacular tie, but where Army and Navy are concerned, it's not only the score on the field that counts. The rivalry goes beyond the goal posts, with each side playing a game of one-upmanship.

Hijinks are always the order of the day.

In the weeks leading up to the 1971 game in Philadelphia, there had been rumors that President Nixon would be in attendance. The day of the game, a limousine drove into JFK Stadium with the presidential flags flapping in the wind and guards running alongside. As the car passed the Cadets, they all stood up stiffly and saluted. The car proceeded to the Navy side, where it stopped in front of the brigade of Midshipmen. When the door opened, the Midshipmen broke into broad smiles. Out stepped the Navy goat, much to the Cadets' chagrin.

The Cadets had every expectation of seeing the president. United States presidents have had a history of attending the game, starting with Teddy Roosevelt in 1901. And it's important for the country's No. 1 citizen to show total objectivity—sitting on one side for the first half and then the other for the second.

Army has had many of its own laughs at Navy's expense. After kidnapping the Navy goat one year, the West Pointers eventually sent the mascot back with a diplomatic escort commanded by a colonel. "I am an adjutant at West Point, have been playing aide to a goat all day, and feel like a bit of an ass," the colonel said as he arrived at Annapolis.

And Navy has laughed back.

In 1991, a group of Midshipmen disguised as Cadets sneaked into the Army infirmary. Their object: kidnap the Army mascot. The intruders tied up the handlers and made off with four Army mules: Spartacus, Trooper, Ranger, and Traveler. As the Midshipmen were fleeing, UH-1 Huey Cobra helicopters gave chase—but too late to run them down.

Back at the Naval Academy, the mules were a featured attraction at the Midshipmen's pep rally. Since then, both sides have officially banned the tradition of mascot kidnappings.

But the nature of the beast has still kept Army and Navy at each other's throats in other ways.

"The Army and the Navy are the best friends in the world 364 and a half days a year," President Eisenhower once said, "but on this one Saturday afternoon, we're the worst of enemies."

1

1926, THE GREATEST OF THEM ALL

Tom Hamilton waited for the snap.

In the gathering dusk of late afternoon, the eyes of 110,000 football fans were on Navy's backfield star as he prepared to kick the extra point.

It was the final minutes of a grim, hard-fought battle with Army. Hamilton's toe could tell the tale for the Naval Academy:

Make the kick and the Middies could preserve their unbeaten record. Miss it and their dreams of a national championship would drown in the muddy, waterlogged turf of Chicago's Soldier Field.

A tight spot was nothing new for Hamilton, who had won more than one game for Navy with his standout kicking ability.

Hamilton had made the previous point-after kicks after Navy's first two touchdowns. Now, if he made the third, the Middies would tie the score at 21.

But, not so fast.

Chicago had been hit by a blizzard the day before. The field had to be cleared of snow which was piled up on the sidelines before the game. It was muddy, and the ball was soggy and hard to grip. And it was getting so dark, it was hard to distinguish the Navy goat from the Army mule. Not exactly the best scenario for a dropkick, the accustomed style of the day.

The dropkick is a long-forgotten art in college football. The kicker has no one to hold the ball in place for him, as in today's game. When the ball was snapped back to Hamilton by the center, he had to catch it, drop it to the field and kick it through the goalposts, all in one smooth motion.

Hamilton was a good kicker, but could he pull it off with a soggy ball under such adverse conditions?

So much breathtaking football action had already been packed into the Army-Navy game of 1926, it was only appropriate that there was still more drama left after nearly three hard-hitting hours.

The fans were huddled in their raccoon coats with thermoses of hot coffee and whiskey to keep them warm.

Among the spectators was the vice president of the United States, Charles Dawes, Mayor Jimmy Walker of New York, and the secretaries of the Navy and War Departments.

They had already witnessed nail-biting excitement with the lead changing hands, and the outcome still in doubt.

The game had featured big plays by big stars—most notably, "Lighthorse" Harry Wilson and Chris Cagle for Army, and Alan Shapley and Hamilton for Navy.

Now it was Army 21, Navy 20 as Hamilton stepped back to make the biggest kick of his career. . . .

Earlier in the season, Hamilton and his Navy team had faced the powerful Michigan Wolverines. In 1925 Fielding Yost's

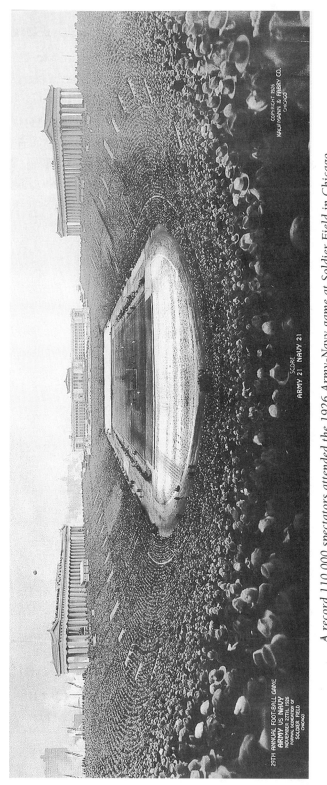

A record 110,000 spectators attended the 1926 Army-Navy game at Soldier Field in Chicago.

Courtesy of the United States Naval Academy

"Point-a-Minute" team just about precisely lived up to its nickname with a 54-0 victory over Navy.

In 1926, the Middies were hoping to make it payback time when the Wolverines came calling in Baltimore.

Point-a-minute Wolverines? Not this time. Not even a point in 60 minutes. Hamilton almost single-handedly made sure of that. On defense he intercepted a pass and batted away another. On offense, the Columbus, Ohio, native kicked a 28-yard field goal in the third period and set up Howard Caldwell's touchdown run in the fourth with a pass off a fake kick.

Final: Navy 10, Michigan 0.

Navy beat nine opponents before the Army game—Purdue, Drake, Richmond, Princeton, Colgate, Michigan, West Virginia Wesleyan, Georgetown, and Loyola—and vaulted into the national championship picture.

The 9-0 record was unexpected. The Middies had lost eight games combined in the previous two years. They were gunning for their first unbeaten season since 1911. And coming into the 1926 Army game, they were looking for their first victory over the Cadets since 1921.

Both Army and Navy had made coaching changes.

In 1926, Bill Ingram replaced Jack Owsley as Navy's head coach. A former backfield star at the Naval Academy, Ingram had coached Indiana University the previous season. Along with Hamilton, Ingram had a group of talented veterans including tackle Frank Wickhorst and running back Shapley.

At West Point, Lawrence M. (Biff) Jones, a star of the great unbeaten 1916 Army team, replaced John McEwan and surrounded himself with former Cadets players as his assistants.

As Jones looked over his squad, he was impressed with the talent, particularly in the backfield. In Wilson, Army had an all-American running back that had already played three years at Penn State.

"In those years they let me play football at West Point even though I had finished a full career at Penn State," Wilson recalled in a 1972 interview. "I think West Point was the only school where I could do that."

He played in some memorable games for Penn State: the 1923 Rose Bowl and a legendary tie with Harvard.

"The first time I got into a game was up at Harvard, halfway through the 1921 season," Wilson recalled. "They had scored twice real quickly and (Coach Hugo) Bezdek didn't look too happy about it. We subs were sitting in open bleachers at the time, and Bezdek turned to me and said, 'Wilson, warm up!'

"I got a little nervous. I got up and ran around and ran around until I got pooped."

Wilson said he was so tired that he had to sit down and rest.

Just as he sat down, Bezdek screamed, "Where's Wilson?"

Wilson showed him. He broke off a 60-yard run as Penn State tied a great Harvard team, 21-21. People were counting on him to do the same at Army.

As a Cadet, Wilson made the team in his first year. Army had no rules then against freshmen playing varsity football. Of course, Wilson was a "freshman" in name only.

The 1926 Army team also featured another great runner in Christian Keener Cagle, otherwise known as Red Cagle. Like Wilson, he became a legend at the Point. Tackle Bud Sprague was another highly regarded Army player.

With those veterans and many other good players, the Cadets boasted one of their strongest teams. One by one, they bounced opponents . . . Detroit . . . Davis & Elkins . . . Syracuse . . . Boston University . . . Yale, and Franklin & Marshall.

Then came Notre Dame, and a 7-0 loss to Knute Rockne's team.

"Notre Dame has a very fast eleven, and we were beaten by

a better team today," Army coach Jones said. "There is no use offering any alibis."

The Cadets then defeated Ursinus before taking on Navy in their traditional season-closer. They had put together an impressive 7-1 record in their first eight games.

Then . . .

Go west, young men. The service academies did.

For the first time, the Army-Navy game would be played in the Midwest. The schools would make history by participating in the first official event at Chicago's Soldier Field, which cost $10 million to build—a hefty sum at the time.

Talk about one of the world's wonders: the stadium encompassed an area a quarter of a mile long and an eighth of a mile wide. The crest was 109 feet above the playing field. There were 85,000 permanent seats, and room for at least 15,000 more in temporary seating. And more room for standing.

And it was more than just another football game. Why, Vice President Dawes would be there to help dedicate the field to the servicemen who had fought in the First World War.

With the crowd expected to be well over 100,000, it would be a record for a college football game. The *New York Times* estimated that between ticket sales to the public and to the two service academies, the gate would be close to $600,000.

"The sum is not alone the largest for any college event, but is also the second largest for any sport," the *Times* reported. "The million-dollar gates at the Dempsey-Carpentier and Dempsey-Firpo heavyweight boxing championships are the only receipts on record that will have eclipsed (the) Army-Navy income."

It was the Roaring Twenties, a wide-open era in America. Cole Porter hadn't yet written his popular classic, "Anything Goes," but that philosophy pretty much reflected the atmosphere of the times. From bathtub gin to the "black bottom" dance craze, anything did go. And everything was bigger than life. That included sports heroes Jack Dempsey, Babe Ruth, and Bill Tilden, and big sports gates at the big events.

And there was no event bigger than the Army-Navy game.

Chicago was a busy, bustling city, welcoming in trainload after trainload of visitors, including the thousands of Cadets and Midshipmen who had come west for the game.

The "Windy City" lived up to its name. Sharp winds and a heavy snowstorm hit the city, leaving a question mark in the minds of many fans whether they wanted to brave sitting on the icy seats in Soldier Field.

Earlier in the week, tickets to the game were in great demand. Scalpers were getting prices as high as $65 and $70 for a $10 "pasteboard." When the weather deteriorated, the scalpers were in a "state of nervous excitement" and prices went down as low as $15.

"Where they were offered at that figure there were no crushes to get them . . . the general public had to thank the weather man for having delivered it from the hands of the exorbitant speculators," the *New York Times* reported.

The day before the game, braving the winds off Lake Michigan and the driving snow, the Cadets and Middies marched down Michigan Avenue to Soldier Field's fabulous new concrete bowl.

It was quite a show.

Meanwhile, the American Legion put on a show of its own. "The Legion section presented a pageant depicting the history of the flag, and behind them were servicemen of allied nations carrying their respective national colors," reported the *Washington Post*. "Thousands formed a human gantlet along Michigan Avenue."

At the stadium, the Army Cadets followed their band onto the field and passed a reviewing stand platoon by platoon. Then, make way for the Navy! "The Vice President, Mayor

Dever, and others of renown lifted ice-encrusted silk hats in recognition," the *Post* said.

Then the military students stood in tight columns in their handsome blue and gray uniforms across the snow-swept field for dedication ceremonies. Thousands more watched from the stands as the vice president delivered the main address.

In the afternoon, the football teams went through their final practices. The Army players did their work indoors, at the South Shore Country Club where they were staying. No indoors for Navy, though. "Undaunted by the rain, sleet and snow, (Navy) traveled from its headquarters at the Hotel Windemere to Stagg Field and romped through a drill that lasted about an hour," reported the *New York Times*.

Both practices were secret. There were cordons of soldiers and sailors posted on guard at each place.

By game time the weather had cleared, the field had been plowed and the snow moved to the sidelines. And the crowds came.

The city bridges were dressed up for the occasion with Army and Navy bunting. The excited crowds descended on Soldier Field. Some 3,000 cops were on duty to make sure that things went smoothly as the pennant-carrying fans entered the fifty entrances to the stadium.

From high society to the man on the street, the fans poured into the stadium. Thousands of others without tickets stood on the great esplanade in front of the field museum and kept their eyes on the illuminated scoreboard to keep in touch with the game.

They were also keeping in touch far out to sea. The Department of the Navy had arranged for the game to be broadcast to ships around the world with the help of a powerful radio station at Annapolis. It was expected the broadcast would be picked up by naval detachments in European waters and naval vessels in the Atlantic, Panama Canal Zone and Caribbean Sea, as well as by naval stations and vessels along the Pacific Coast of the United States.

Meanwhile, the nation's No. 1 fan, President Calvin Coolidge, also kept in touch by radio. He set aside his presidential duties for a few hours. Governing the country could wait for Army-Navy.

Navy coach Ingram had some advice for his Cadets before they took the field, as Hamilton would later recall: "In going out for your warm-ups, I want you to stop at the end of the runway and look as long as you want at the largest crowd ever to witness a football game, 110,000 people, and then to forget the crowd."

The game began. . . .

Using a Knute Rockne tactic, Army coach Jones started his second-string team to "soften up" the Middies. His plan was to bring in the first team later to deliver the knockout punch.

The tactic backfired. Navy rammed the ball from midfield to the Army 2-yard line, and Caldwell hurled himself into the end zone. Hamilton's extra point made it 7-0.

Early in the second period, J. B. Shuber burst over right tackle from two yards out to cap a 66-yard drive for the Middies. Hamilton, who set up the score with a 36-yard pass to Harry Hardwick, drop-kicked another extra point for a 14-0 lead.

It looked like it was going to be Navy all the way. Suddenly, things were going the other way.

In the second period, Wilson scored on a 17-yard dash through tackle, capping a four-play, 65-yard drive for Army.

Later in the period, Army punted to Navy. The ball hit the arm of Navy safety Howard Ransford, and the pigskin careened backward, rolling to the Middies' 25-yard line.

Army end Norris Harbold, in his haste to grab the ball, crashed into Ransford. Harbold picked himself off the turf, and streaked toward the ball, which had rolled to the 15-yard line.

"His fingers were cold and he had a hard time wrapping them around the leather," said the New York Times. "At the five-yard line, he lost his balance and fell. He picked himself up, tottered another few feet, and went down again. This time he decided that crawling was better than running, and on hands and knees, he sprawled along until he was over the goal line.

"All of which proves again that an army travels on its stomach."

The Times said the Army stands "went wild with boisterous enthusiasm. Lighthorse Harry Wilson booted a placement kick that left this epic as even as it was before the kick-off."

The score at the half: 14-14.

Between the halves, it looked like the Social Hour on the field.

"Chauncey McCormick and his young son, Brooks, were tramping up and down to warm up, having left Mrs. McCormick with their blankets," reported the New York Times.

"Mrs. Albert R. Brunker, in a leopard skin coat, green woolen stockings and high galoshes, and Mr. Brunker were walking and chatting with friends."

The halftime show featured a mock battle between a "cruiser" and a "tank," both cleverly built on automobile chassis. They raced around the field, firing shots at each other. However, the more compelling battle was to come in the second half.

The Cadets took the kickoff at the start of the third quarter and drove seventy-six yards for a touchdown and a 21-14 lead. Cagle led the charge with a brilliant 43-yard scoring run.

Not so fast, Army.

Back came Navy. In the descending darkness on a field framed with piles of snow, the Middies put on a desperate drive.

"An aerial attack, which had puzzled the soldiers all day, again sent the Navy horde down the field and amid a frenzied *cheering from the Midshipmen section, Navy battered its way through for the touchdown,"* said the New York Times.

This time, it was Shapley who scored from the 8-yard line on a tricky double-reverse play.

But, wait, Navy still needed Hamilton's extra-point kick to tie.

Hamilton wiped mud from his booted toe, then set himself and took the pass from center.

"The field was almost as silent as a tomb," noted an observer. *"The Middies in the East stands were holding their breath. The Cadets were indulging in silent prayers."*

This was pressure—but Hamilton had been in tight spots before. So what did he do? He simply drop-kicked the ball straight through the uprights for a 21-21 tie.

The Midshipmen in the stands were on their feet, cheering wildly.

There was still time for the Cadets to pull it out. Led by the ubiquitous Wilson, Army stormed to the Navy 16-yard line in the closing minutes. From there, Wilson tried a field goal, but it was wide of the target. The titanic struggle ended in a 21-21 tie.

"Brave rallies and gallant stands, drama, suspense, thrills—all these were packed into the game until the senses were bewildered," James R. Harrison wrote in the *New York Times*.

The florid description was typical of the exaggerated writing in those days. But for once, the football game actually matched the journalists' hyperbolic prose.

2

THE BEGINNINGS, THE 1890s

It was a cold, gloomy day in November when a cheerful group of football players from the Naval Academy arrived at West Point for a game with Army.

Up the hill from the Hudson River they flowed, broad-shouldered and trim, with a goat in tow. The Midshipmen had picked up the animal along the way and decided to keep it as their "mascot."

When they reached the playing field, the Navy men were greeted by a crowd of excited spectators and a squad of Army football players.

The date: November 29, 1890.

The place: the parade grounds at West Point, otherwise known as "The Plain."

The occasion: the first Army-Navy football game.

If there had been oddsmakers or football pools in those days, the game probably would have been off the charts.

All the smart money would have been on Navy, which had

been playing intercollegiate football since 1879 and continuously since 1882. The Army team? This was the Cadets' very first appearance in a football game against another school.

If not for Dennis Mahan Michie, it might have taken Army longer to get into intercollegiate football. Michie knew and loved the game, having played it at Lawrenceville Academy. More importantly, Michie knew a leading member of the academic board that set school policy at West Point—his father.

The board had been dead set against football at the academy, branding it as a "frivolous distraction." But Michie's family connection got him the green light to make a date with Navy, answering a sharp challenge from the Midshipmen.

The football equipment of the day was so rudimentary it was laughable by modern standards. The players had only a few extra layers of canvas on their bodies for protection. The "headgear" consisted of a heavy growth of hair—the players had no haircuts during the season—and a stocking cap.

According to one newspaper account of the day, the Middies came on the field with red and white stocking caps and red stockings. The Cadet players wore black and orange caps, white suits and black stockings.

That same account noted that there was a crowd of "a hundred-odd" at the game. Another report said it was more like 1,000 spectators.

After winning the toss and getting the ball, Navy went into a V-wedge formation.

"Reef the topsail!" Navy quarterback Moulton Johnson shouted.

The Army players were puzzled. Then they were pummeled as Navy came running at them behind a big line shaped like a V. Chalk up a big gain for Navy halfback Charles (Red) Emerich.

On the next play, the Navy quarterback yelled at the top of

The 1890 Navy team that played in the first Army-Navy game.
Courtesy of the United States Naval Academy

his voice: "Stand by to clear anchor!" Once more, it was Navy gobbling up big chunks of yardage. The Army Cadets were helpless before the great Navy surge.

This was all too common a scene on The Plain that day. Navy seemed to know what it was doing. Army didn't have a clue.

On one play, an Army tackle grabbed a Navy running back and spun him around. The spectators standing on the edge of the field cheered. But the Army tackle thought they were voicing their disapproval, so he let the runner go. And the runner did go—right toward the Army goal line.

"I thought I had done something wrong," the befuddled Army tackle said.

Noted one contemporary account of the first Army-Navy game:

> Navy's stalwarts, from the kickoff, were too much for the deadly ignorant Cadets, and with charges around the ends and center rushes which the West Pointers tried to stop with might and main, succeeded in rolling rough shod over them.
>
> Emerich scored most of the touchdowns for Navy, while Michie gave a good account of himself for the Military Academy. He was the only Cadet who has played football before.

Emerich finished with twenty points—touchdowns were worth four points then—and Moulton added another touchdown as Navy swamped Army, 24-0.

All was not lost for Army, though.

"After the game the Cadets entertained the Midshipmen at a dance," a newspaper reported, "and the affair ended in an enjoyable day for all."

The following season, Army had a more experienced team and a better ground game. Led by Elmer Clark, the Cadets overpowered the Midshipmen, 32-16.

When news of the result reached West Point, the captain of the corps assembled the Cadets and announced:

"Final score! Army 32, Navy 16. Dismiss your companies!"

The celebration was on. The Cadets marched around the post. The band played, guns were fired (eleven, one for each member of the team) and "bonfires were lighted with fine effect," according to one report.

A rivalry was born. The greatest of all football rivalries was born.

While it didn't have the spectacular trappings of the present day, the Army-Navy game even then brought out the best—and sometimes the worst—of those involved.

Take the 1893 game, witnessed by 10,000 at Annapolis. The Middies beat Army 6-4 to take a 3-1 lead in the series.

The bigger story was what happened in the stands. There, a brigadier general and a rear admiral got into a heated argument and challenged each other to a duel.

It's uncertain whether the duel ever came off. But President Grover Cleveland was angry enough to order the series stopped. It wasn't until 1899 that it was resumed. By that time, it was shifted to a neutral site, Franklin Field in Philadelphia.

Army pulled off the first upset of the rivalry with a 17-5 win over a Navy team that had shut out its three previous opponents by a combined 71-0 score.

A decade was coming to a close. The "Gay Nineties," as the 1890s has sometimes been called, was in many ways anything but that.

It was a wild, roller-coaster ride for many Americans.

There was financial panic—a stock market crash and a depression in 1893 when 600 banks failed, one-third of the nation's railroads went broke and 15,000 businesses went bankrupt.

There was war. The sinking of an American battleship in

the harbor off Cuba inspired the phrase, "Remember the Maine" and set off the Spanish-American War in 1898.

There were race issues, a division between the nation's white and black leaders. There were lynchings of blacks by white southerners. The state of Mississippi, for one, limited civil rights for blacks.

But there was also hope. In 1896 gold was discovered in the Yukon territory of Canada, sparking the great North American Gold Rush.

And there were important inventions. Thomas A. Edison patented his kinetoscope, a camera which took moving pictures on strips of film. And James A. Naismith invented a new sport called basketball.

The Army-Navy football series, meanwhile, was ready to continue its own roller-coaster ride.

3

INNOVATORS AND THE ROUGH RIDER, 1900-1909

He was the Galloping Ghost before there was a Galloping Ghost, the Gipper before there was a Gipper, the Golden Boy before there was a Golden Boy.

Long before Red Grange tore up football fields at Illinois and George Gipp did so at Notre Dame, and much longer before Paul Hornung won the Heisman Trophy with the Fighting Irish, there was Charley Daly with the Army football team.

Before becoming a successful Army coach, Daly was one of football's first superstars in the early 1900s. And the dynamic little quarterback could boast of an accomplishment that none of the other three football legends could claim: Daly won all-American honors at not one but two schools, Harvard and Army.

Because of this, Daly was the center of a controversy.

Navy wanted Army to tighten its eligibility rules for athletes. Army permitted Cadets to enter up to the age of twenty-one, allowing experienced players like Daly to join and make an immediate impact on the football program.

Navy thought this gave Army an unfair advantage, because Navy only accepted students up to the age of twenty.

Army stood firm—for the time being. In later years, the service academies signed an agreement that anyone with more than three years of football experience at another school could not play in Army-Navy games.

As for Daly, *he* seemed to save his best for the Navy game.

In 1901, Daly became legendary at the Point when he set an Army record with a 100-yard kickoff return as the Cadets beat Navy 11-5. With his field goal and extra-point kicking, Daly accounted for all of Army's points.

The following year, Daly was again the star of the game with his quarterbacking, kicking, and running. When the Middies threatened to rally late in the game, Daly scored the clinching touchdown in Army's 22-8 triumph.

Because of the eligibility controversy, Daly decided after the 1902 season not to play at West Point again.

The Middies were glad to see Daly go, although they still couldn't beat Army. At least, not until the 1906 season, when they went airborne with the revolutionary forward pass.

The aerial game was appropriate for a turn-of-the-century decade that featured the first flight by the rigid-framed "zeppelin," named after count Ferdinand von Zeppelin, and the first airplane flight of the Wright brothers.

Things were moving faster along the ground in the "Ragtime Era." It was goodbye to horse-drawn carriages and hello to vehicles powered by electricity and gas.

For the Army-Navy football series, it was full speed ahead, as well.

The rivalry was starting to draw the attention of an entire nation. When the Cadets and Middies met in Philadelphia's

Franklin Field in 1901, upward of 25,000 fans attended. And tickets were being scalped for $40.

Among the spectators was Theodore Roosevelt, who had moved into the White House following the assassination of President McKinley in 1901.

Roosevelt was an old Army man, but he rooted enthusiastically for both sides. At the 1901 game, he sat on the Navy side during the first half and then switched to Army's in the second, the start of a long-standing tradition for United States presidents.

When Navy tied the score 5-5, Roosevelt was so excited he leaped out of his seat, broke clear of his security guards and made a mad dash to the Middies bench, where he slapped the players on their backs.

In the 1905 game played in Princeton, New Jersey, Roosevelt once more prowled the sidelines and cheered on the teams. He became so animated at one point that his security people had to practically restrain him from running on the field.

Roosevelt, a hardy outdoors type who fought in the Spanish-American War, loved football. But he didn't like what was happening to the sport, which was suddenly the center of controversy with an unusual number of deaths and injuries. In 1905, there were more than twenty football fatalities and a number of serious injuries, and many colleges had banned the sport.

One player remembered how violent the game was in the early 1900s, especially for quarterbacks.

"He'd have these large loops on his belt and a teammate on each side of him would hoist him up and throw him over the line," recalled Dutch Herman, who played for Penn State in the early 1900s. "They lost a lot of quarterbacks that way."

Roosevelt had seen other things in the game he didn't like. Once, attending a major Eastern game, the president witnessed a player biting away a piece of an opponent's ear.

Roosevelt was outraged. He considered banning the sport altogether.

Instead, he invited "Skinny Paul" Dashiell, the Navy coach from 1904 to 1906, and Army captain Palmer Pierce to the White House to discuss what could be done about the increasing violence in the game.

That meeting was the catalyst for rules changes that would eventually transform the murderous rugby style of football's early days into the modern game. This included the elimination of mass momentum plays such as the deadly "Flying Wedge."

But even though the Flying Wedge was outlawed, football could still be extremely dangerous. There were "mass plays" that were offspring of the Wedge and still considered legal.

In the 1909 season, Army met Harvard at West Point before a crowd of about 10,000. One of the onlookers was John Byrne, father of Cadet mainstay Eugene Byrne.

Byrne weighed only 170 pounds, but like many of his Army teammates was a real scrapper. The Cadets at that time may have not had the biggest or most talented group of players, but they were certainly a battling group.

Harvard, led by two-time all-American tackle Hamilton Fish Jr., had it all: size, strength, and talent. Fish was a specimen at six foot four, 200 pounds.

The Crimson were considered the No. 2 team in the East behind only mighty Yale. At that time, being No. 2 in the East was virtually the same as being No. 2 in the country. It was a time when the Ivy League, particularly the "Big Three" of Yale, Harvard, and Princeton, ruled college football.

On this fall afternoon, Harvard was cruising with a 9-0 lead late in the game.

With only about 10 minutes left, Harvard called for a "mass" play—sending fullback Wayne Minot crashing through the line behind the stout interference of Fish and Robert Fisher. The play was directed at a space on the line between Byrne and Vern Purnell.

The big bodies of the Harvard line cracked into the smaller Army line. Byrne, wearing the thin leather helmet of the day that offered little protection, lunged forward and then disappeared underneath a twisting mass of arms and legs. When everything cleared, both Byrne and Minot lay motionless on the ground.

Minot was quickly revived, as the *New York Times* reported. He "regained his feet after his face had been washed and a little water poured down his throat."

Byrne, however, was not so lucky. Efforts by several Army surgeons and the team trainer failed to revive him. Byrne's father had left his seat in the cheering section to be with his son on the field.

After a while, the twenty-one-year-old Byrne was carried off the field and brought to the Army infirmary, barely breathing. Doctors used artificial respiration and oxygen to keep him alive.

Miraculously, around midnight Byrne woke from unconsciousness and talked intermittently with his father and others throughout the night. But by dawn, Byrne had died of a dislocated vertebrae and spine injuries.

Byrne was one of thirty-three football-related deaths reported across the country in 1909.

Army immediately canceled the last four games of the season, including the meeting with Navy.

About this time, the forward pass was becoming an important part of the game.

Now the ball could be thrown forward to an eligible receiver. No longer did quarterbacks have to fly through the air with the greatest of unease.

Dashiell was among those chiefly responsible for the introduction of the forward pass. The new weapon was much in evidence when Dashiell's Navy team played Army in 1906.

When a fumbled punt gave Navy the ball on the Army 40-yard line, Homer Norton dropped back as if to try a field goal. Instead, he lofted a pass to Jonas Ingram and the Navy receiver ran past the flabbergasted Cadets for a touchdown.

With "Anchors Away" making its debut, the Middies were inspired by the rousing new school song and beat the Cadets 10-0.

The Middies followed with a 6-0 triumph in 1907, and were 10-to-7 favorites to beat Army again in 1908. The fans at Franklin Field got their money's worth watching one of the great early battles in the Army-Navy series.

Army scored first. Navy's Ed Lange fumbled a kick and Army's Henry Chamberlain, who would later become an Olympic equestrian, picked up the ball and ran to the 3-yard line. Bill Dean plunged over for a touchdown (then worth five points) and kicked the extra point for a 6-0 Army lead.

Back came Navy as Lange returned a punt from midfield to the Army 25. Lange alternated with H. M. Clay and John Dalton to move the ball to the Army 6.

The Cadets' defense tightened, forcing Navy to kick a field goal. Lange booted the ball through the uprights for the four-pointer.

Both defenses were impenetrable from that point, and the result was a 6-4 upset victory for Army. The closeness of the game was revealed in the stats: Navy made only three first downs, and Army two.

The tight battle was an indication of things to come.

4

STOP DALTON! STOP OLIPHANT!

1910-1919

Just call him "Three-to-Nothing" Jack Dalton.

When the Army-Navy game resumed following the one-year hiatus because of Byrne's death, Dalton was the offense and nothing but the whole offense for the Middies for two years running.

The score of the 1910 game: Navy 3, Army 0.

The score of the 1911 game: Navy 3, Army 0.

Both years, Dalton's field goals were the difference in these great defensive battles between the service academies.

Dalton was the difference in other ways. On a windy day in the 1910 clash, Dalton's thunderous punts continually put the Middies in good field position as they completed their first un beaten season.

And in 1911, the Navy fullback and captain made a couple of long runs and a 72-yard punt along with his game-winning kick.

In 1912, the Middies again used the field goal to top the Cadets. This time it was Babe Brown, later to become a distinguished admiral, who did the damage. He kicked two through the uprights for a 6-0 Middies victory, their third straight shutout in the series.

Not to be outdone, Army then won the next four games, two of them by shutouts. In 1914, the Cadets posted their first unbeaten season at 9-0, including a 20-0 pasting of Navy.

The Cadets could thank Elmer Oliphant for a lot of their success—and not just in football—in the next few years.

Oliphant did it all for Army—pass, run, kick, block, and tackle. He was Bo Jackson before there was a Bo Jackson, only more diversified.

Fans cheer as the Middies top the Cadets 6-0 in 1912.
Bettmann/CORBIS

While at the Point, Oliphant not only won all-American honors in football, he also won letters in basketball, baseball, and track. When he had some spare time, he participated in boxing, hockey, and swimming.

In 1915, the first Army-Navy game with the players wearing numbers for identification purposes, Oliphant scored two touchdowns and kicked two extra points.

Final: Army 14, Navy 0.

In 1916, Army featured one of its great early teams. While Oliphant at times seemed like the whole Cadets team, he was not.

The Cadets also featured such greats as Cap McEwan, Biff Jones, Charley Gerhardt, Babe Weyand, and Bruce (Bruiser) Butler.

But before the Army-Navy game of that year, the Middies could only think of one man. They remembered what Oliphant had done to them the year before.

The orders of the day at the Naval Academy the morning of the 1916 game: "6 a.m.—Rise; Stop Oliphant: 7 a.m.— Breakfast; Stop Oliphant."

The Middies could not.

On the first play of the game, Oliphant raced eighty-five yards to the Navy 5-yard line. Three plays later, Oliphant plunged over for the touchdown.

Later in the period, Oliphant kicked a field goal. Then in the second quarter it was Oliphant carrying the ball on most of the plays as Army made an extended drive for another touchdown.

It was another Army win, 15-7.

It was the last time Oliphant would compete against Navy. The 1917 season was cut short by the First World War, and the Army-Navy game canceled. It wouldn't be played again until

1919, when Navy finally ended years of frustration with a 6-0 victory.

After that game at the Polo Grounds in New York, the ecstatic Middies marched up and down the field. As they crossed under one of the goalposts, they threw their hats over the crossbars and sang, "The End of a Perfect Day."

It was not nearly so perfect in terms of world events. The years between 1910 and 1919 had been filled with violence: a revolutionary war in Mexico and a world war for the United States that threatened the free world. The "Red Baron," the German flying ace, caused problems for Allied pilots in the first aerial battles ever witnessed before he was finally brought down, along with his country.

By the time the decade ended, there were notable achievements in aviation, including incredible transatlantic flights.

By 1920, the Army-Navy football rivalry was also about to reach new heights.

5

ROARING RIVALRY, 1920-1929

In the final minutes of the 1926 Army-Navy game, there was a typical scene on the sidelines:

Navy captain Frank Wickhorst had called timeout and gathered his teammates around him.

Pointing to the distant goal line, Wickhorst said: "We are going across that goal line without losing the ball. Let's go!"

The Middies plunged, plowed, and scrapped sixty-five yards for a touchdown and a thrilling 21-21 tie with Army.

Because so much was at stake and there was so much focus on that game in Chicago, it's generally regarded as the greatest in the Army-Navy series.

But the 1920s alone produced a number of other epic battles between the service academies that could give the 1926 classic a run for its money.

Try 1922, for one.

The game was back at Franklin Field in Philadelphia after

five straight years at the Polo Grounds in New York and three straight shutouts by Navy. And the place was packed with 55,000 fans.

The lead changed hands four times and the game wasn't decided until the fourth quarter. Navy led 14-10 when Army's George Smythe ran back a punt fifty yards to the Middies' 10.

The Cadets tried some running plays, but were pushed back thirteen yards by the hard-working Navy defense. Finally Smythe threw a touchdown pass to Fran Dodd for a 17-14 Army win.

Try 1923, for another.

While there was no scoring in this game at the muddy Polo Grounds, there was plenty of exciting action.

Army twice blocked Navy punts in the shadow of the Middies' goalposts, but failed to recover them. Under rules of the day, the Middies retained possession both times.

Army had another scoring opportunity, but kicking star Ed Garbisch narrowly missed a 35-yard field goal try.

Navy had a chance to break the scoreless tie when S. G. Barchet intercepted an Army pass. There was only one Army defender in position to stop him from going all the way. Finally, after a 40-yard run, Barchet was brought down on the 26 by William Wood, a former teammate at Johns Hopkins.

Or try consecutive 7-0 shutouts by Navy in 1920 and 1921, a 10-3 victory by Army in 1925, and a 14-9 triumph by the Cadets in 1927.

Just about every game in the 1920s was fiercely competitive between the service academies. Of the eight played in the decade, only one was decided by more than seven points.

And most were defensive classics. From 1920–1927, neither team scored more than seventeen points except in the 21-21 tie. The loser was blanked three times and there was the scoreless tie in 1923.

Players shake hands during the 1923 game.
Bettmann/CORBIS

This was during the "Golden Age" of sports, with such heroic athletic figures as Babe Ruth, Bill Tilden, Bobby Jones, Red Grange, and Jack Dempsey.

But it was also the golden age for the Army-Navy series, which produced some of the most unforgettable games between the two schools. Arguably the rivalry came of age in this decade known as the Roaring Twenties.

Famed sportswriter Grantland Rice christened the Army-Navy rivalry the "biggest show on earth."

At times, it seemed even bigger than that. And not even cancellation of the 1928 and 1929 games because of eligibility differences could change that.

The Navy team rests on the sideline during the 1923 game.
Bettman/CORBIS

From the president to the man on the street, the rivalry drew nationwide attention and overflow crowds—including a college football record 110,000 at Chicago's Soldier Field in 1926.

The 1920s featured some of the rivalry's all-time greats. For Army, there were "Lighthorse" Harry Wilson, Chris Cagle, Bud Sprague, Laverne (Blondie) Saunders, Garrison Davidson and Garbisch. For Navy, there were Wickhorst, Tom Hamilton, Alan Shapley, Howard Caldwell, Tom Eddy, and Hank Hardwick.

Many of them later became stars of another kind. Hamilton, for one, would become a Navy coach and a wartime admiral. Wickhorst worked with Hamilton to set up the renowned Navy preflight program during the Second World War.

Wilson, the Army team captain in 1927, would also distinguish himself in the war. He commanded a B-25 bombing group that flew forty-eight missions in the Pacific and retired as an Air Force colonel.

In the 1920s, war was the furthest thing from any of their minds. The United States was still recovering from the First World War—and doing quite nicely, at first. There were great economic advances in the country in the early part of the decade.

But such prosperity ended with the stock market crash in 1929. That brought uncertain times to America, and around the world.

As for the Army-Navy game, there was nothing uncertain about it. Army-Navy had become one of the great sports spectacles in the country.

6

CRASHES AND CROWD-PLEASERS, 1930-1939

Tom Hamilton had been through this agony before.

In 1926, Hamilton kicked the crucial extra point as Navy tied Army 21-21 in the game many consider the greatest in the rivalry.

In 1934, Hamilton was back at Navy as the coach and once more involved in a tight game with Army.

There were other similarities:

Like Soldier Field in Chicago eight years earlier, the weather conditions at Franklin Field in Philadelphia were treacherous.

And once again, a kick of a water-logged ball decided the outcome.

This time, it was Slade Cutter's 28-yard field goal through a driving rainstorm in the first quarter that lifted the Middies to a 3-0 victory over the Cadets.

Along with Cutter, Fred "Buzz" Borries also starred for

Navy. He ran the ball into position for Cutter's field goal, among his other duties that day.

"Borries made about ten last-man tackles in that game," noted E. E. "Rip" Miller, who was an assistant coach for Navy in 1934 after serving as head coach for three straight years.

The weather wasn't fit for fowl or football player.

The *Annapolis Lucky Bag*, part of the print media, described how Navy took a timeout "and made careful preparations for wiping off the ball and Slade Cutter's shoe . . . and then, from the 20-yard line, Bill Clark holding the ball, Slade sent it squarely between the uprights, accomplishing what had seemed almost impossible: Navy 3, Army 0. And that completed the scoring for the afternoon."

Statistics told the story of that dreary day: the teams combined for a grand total of 132 yards and made only five first downs between them. They also combined to throw eight passes, completing three of them. And Army and Navy punted a total of twenty-five times!

Maybe it wasn't a pretty win, and the conditions weren't all that great, but to the Middies it was a beautiful day. And the perfect outcome.

It was their first victory over Army since 1921—a stretch of ten games, the longest non-winning record for either team in the series. During that period, the Cadets had won eight times and there were two ties.

The rivalry had resumed in 1930 following a feud over eligibility requirements that cancelled two games. And the Cadets picked up where they had left off with a 6-0 victory.

Despite the depressed economy following the stock market crash, Army-Navy games continued to sell out, as did a lot of sporting events.

Fans flocked to the games, as they did to movies, as a respite from their troubles. No matter what, there always seemed to be enough money for entertainment to escape the dreariness of the everyday world. For a couple of hours, at least, they could cheer on their favorite team and forget about all their problems at home.

When Army and Navy clashed in 1930, a jam-packed crowd welcomed them back in their first game at Yankee Stadium in New York.

These were also lush times for the Army football teams, which were mauling some opponents by scores of 60-0 and 67-6 and winning a major portion of their games through the 1930s.

Predicated mainly on defense, the Cadets posted twenty-eight shutouts in the first four seasons of the 1930s. They finished with a 71-22-5 record for the decade, including 7-3 versus Navy.

The 1933 team, featuring Harvey Jablonsky at guard, was one of Army's truly greatest. The Cadets won their first nine games, including 12-7 over Navy. That, incidentally, was only the second touchdown Army had allowed all season.

All systems were go for a perfect season and a possible national championship. The Cadets were leading Notre Dame 12-0 with less than 10 minutes to play in the final game when they had a shocking, inexplicable letdown. The Irish rallied for a 13-12 victory to spoil Army's perfection and its shot at national glory.

Jablonsky would be voted into the College Football Hall of Fame, but more than likely would have given up that honor for another crack at the Fighting Irish.

Tackle Jack Price, who made the all-American team in 1930 and 1931, was another big Army star of the period. Other featured players included guard Milt Summerfelt, running back Jack Buckler, end Bill Shuler, and tackle Harry Stella.

It wasn't until 1939 that Army had a losing season—its first in thirty-three years. By then, coach Bill Wood was in his second season after replacing the successful Gar Davidson.

While the Middies didn't have half the success in the decade that Army had, they did have their moments in a period featuring a 48-40-6 record.

There was, of course, that dramatic 1934 win over Army starring Borries and Cutter, Navy's only all-American representatives of the decade. Also a 7-0 victory over Army in 1936 in the first of many games played in Philadelphia's Municipal Stadium.

And then there was 1939. Although this was not one of the strongest of Cadets teams, the Middies were still the underdogs. Coming into the game, they had not managed to win a major game all season.

That didn't bother Emory "Swede" Larson, the new Navy coach who had some tricks up his sleeve. Actually, an old blanket in the storehouse.

A star on Navy teams from 1919–1921, Larson had never lost to Army as a player. He was determined not to do so as a coach, either.

What did he do? He pulled out an old blanket worn by Navy's mascot goat in 1921 and adorned Billy VIII, the present mascot, with the same blanket.

And magic seemed to happen on the field as Navy drilled Army 10-0 to put the cap on a tumultuous decade.

The 1930s began with a focus on economic recovery following the stock market crash and ended with a preoccupation with the drums of war in Europe.

Soon, many of the same players who battled in the Army-Navy games of the 1930s would be thrust head-first into a much more important battle: the Second World War.

7

MR. INSIDE AND MR. OUTSIDE, 1940-1949

College football would lose some of its luster in the 1940s, when war raged around the globe, taking many of the young athletes from campuses to battle zones.

Not surprisingly, though, two schools that consistently could field strong teams during the Second World War were Army and Navy.

With the Great Lakes Naval Training Center and the Army Air Corps at Randolph Field attracting some of the finest athletes in America, both Army and Navy prospered on the football field. By mid-decade, West Point would be the home of the most dynamic duo in the sport's history: Glenn (Mr. Outside) Davis and Felix "Doc" (Mr. Inside) Blanchard.

But before they emerged as Heisman Trophy winners, the Army-Navy rivalry and the teams themselves would have a significant impact on the jumbled sporting landscape.

In 1940, with the United States hoping to remain out of the conflict in Europe, the rivalry's fiftieth game drew the likes of the Secretaries of War and the Navy, the Joint Chiefs of Staff, and highest-ranking officers of both services to Philadelphia.

Also in attendance was William Whiskers VII, Navy's billy goat mascot, who emerged from an armored car, escorted by four armed guards.

Pageantry was particularly in evidence for this game, including a rousing rendition of the final portion of "Columbia, the Gem of the Ocean," featuring the lyrics "Army and Navy forever, three cheers for the red, white and blue."

The game itself didn't live up to the enhanced festivities. Navy simply was the better team and its defense never allowed the Cadets to march downfield. Indeed, when the Middies took a 7-0 lead in the opening minutes, it was more than enough. The Middies won 14-0, their second straight shutout and third in five years in the series.

The key player for Navy was "Barnacle" Bill Busik, who would go on to become a naval commander and, in the 1960s, the athletic director at Annapolis. Busik not only was an offensive force, but he also handled many special teams duties.

And the coach was Emory "Swede" Larson, who never lost to Army during his career as a center, then as coach at Navy. When Larson took over as head coach in 1939, he placed the following credo on a sign in the team's locker room: "It can, it shall be done. Beat Army."

He always was true to his vow. "Swede was a real softhearted guy with a great personality," Busik later explained. "He was nervous as the dickens before any game. He was more nervous than we were, but he'd relax us. He was a tough Marine. He knew how to lead out there."

In 1941, Larson led the Middies in his final game at the academy. He sensed what was ahead as the teams suited up on

November 29, 1941. Little did he know how soon his expectations would be realized.

Army, coached for the first time by Earl "Red" Blaik, was more successful than the previous two years because it actually scored, taking a 6-0 lead at halftime. That didn't seem to worry the Middies.

One of them was Bob Woods, who played in the next two classics as well for Army. "Fox Movietone reelmen, reporters, they stuck their heads into the dressing room," said Woods. "They said, 'We've got to know which side to set the cameras on. Who's going to win?'

"We said, 'You set 'em up on this side. We're going to win.' Then we went out and scored two successive touchdowns and won the game."

Busik again was the catalyst. Not only did he nail a 77-yard punt, but with the offense stymied by a staunch Cadets defense, he was the key component in a bit of trickery. Larson ordered an end run, but quarterback Wes Gebert improvised. He called a double reverse, and the ball ended up in Busik's hands. From the Navy 30, he sped to the Army 1, and the Middies scored moments later to take the lead.

They would not be caught.

"It was wonderful to see how well the boys responded," Larson said. Then, with the jubilant Middies celebrating their third straight win over the Cadets, Larson announced his immediate plans: "This is my last game of football for a while, boys. There's a bigger game coming up, and I aim to be right in it."

And he was. He was awarded four battle stars during the war, then became the chief of Marines special services. He even was offered a job coaching and overseeing sports at the University of Washington, but Larson died in 1945 of a heart attack.

Among his mementos was a coverlet on which was inscribed the years and scores of the Army-Navy games Larson participated in. And a special ball.

"When we beat Army in '41, on the train we took the game ball and we all autographed it and gave it to him," Busik recalled. "Years later, his widow gave me that ball when I became the athletic director. I kept it on my desk, then on our fiftieth reunion of the team in '91 I gave that ball back to the Naval Academy."

Eight days after Navy's 1941 victory, while the Midshipmen were being saluted at the academy for their win, Pearl Harbor was attacked. What was planned as a day of acclamation instead became that Day of Infamy. Hundreds of athletes from the academies soon were plunged into war on two fronts: Europe and the Pacific.

There even was some talk of abandoning athletics at the academies to concentrate solely on preparing young men for war. But the superintendents at West Point and Annapolis felt that was the absolutely wrong approach, and General Francis B. Wilby appeared before the House Appropriations Committee to convince the Senate of the importance of sports at the schools.

"All of us feel it would be a very sad day if athletics were abandoned at West Point," the superintendent for the academy said. "The body contact types are one of the finest things in the training of a soldier."

That training became far more intense, and many football players—particularly upperclassmen—had difficulty with their schedules. Some weeks, they would be training locally in airplanes or on ships or doing maneuvers, in addition to the class work and football practices.

The strain showed on some, but most found football as something of a respite. And with freshmen now eligible to play during the war, coaches had fresh legs to push the juniors and seniors.

Blaik was turning around Army's football fortunes, but not when it came to the biggest game. Navy was on a three-year winning streak when the Cadets traveled to Annapolis for the 1942 meeting.

While President Franklin Delano Roosevelt had plenty else to keep him occupied, he encouraged universities "to continue playing your games for the morale boost it provides a nation much in need of one."

No schools could provide more of a boost than the academies, and when they met for the first time during the war, it

Earl Blaik (left) looks on from the bench.
Courtesy of the United States Military Academy

was an eerie scene. The game was moved to Thompson Stadium in Annapolis for security purposes. Organizers reasoned that a gathering of 100,000 people for a game involving the military academies and attended by both the Corps and the Brigade—not to mention assorted generals and admirals—was too inviting a target. So a crowd estimated at anywhere from 10,000 to 15,000, mostly locals because of travel restrictions during the war, showed up.

Not there: the Corps of Cadets, which was prohibited from journeying to the game. Instead, about half of the Brigade was ordered to cheer for Army, a command about as popular as asking the Middies not to salute the flag.

To make such an order even more distasteful, the Black Knights of the Hudson brought a winning record to Annapolis and surely were a threat to end Navy's recent dominance of the series.

"We were making progress toward our goals," Blaik said. "We had developed a highly competitive team that was capable of facing any opponent and providing a formidable challenge."

But the challenge of winning at Navy with no true rooting section and against a team that, in recent seasons at least, had the Cadets' number, was too daunting. The Army cheering section of third-class and fourth-class Midshipmen willingly sang the Army fight song, but when it came to actually cheering for the Cadets, well, suffice to say there was little merriment.

But there was plenty of celebrating in Annapolis after a 14-0 win that was Navy's third shutout of Army in four years. Indeed, defense had become so surpassing that from 1936 through 1942, neither team scored more than fourteen points and the loser was shut out five times.

Blaik was beaten in that game by John "Billick" Whelchel, who had been recalled from active duty to coach the Middies.

Whelchel was a Navy quarterback from 1916–1918, losing the only Army-Navy game in that span.

He then shuttled between commanding such ships as the USS *Louisville, Texas,* and *Hannibal* and coaching at the academy. He always had his hand in football, working at Annapolis under several head coaches and guiding teams at various Navy yards and on several ships. After returning to Annapolis in 1941 as athletic director, Whelchel also worked with Larson. And when Larson set off to war in 1942—as Whelchel also planned to do—he instead replaced the Swede as coach.

Whelchel's head-coaching term would last only two years. Then he would become chief of staff to the Commander Service Squadron in the Pacific theater. As an admiral, Whelchel oversaw assaults on Iwo Jima and on Okinawa as commander of the USS *San Francisco,* winning a Legion of Merit award, a Gold Star, and a Bronze Star.

In 1949, he became the first Washington, D.C., native to coach the Redskins, although his stay lasted all of seven games (3-3-1 record).

Whelchel would win his only other contest against Army as Navy coach, 13-0 in 1943. It would be Navy's last win against its archrival in the decade.

Going into the 1943 game, in the heart of the war, Navy was hoping to equal Army's streak of five victories from 1927–1933—the longest in the series to that point. The Middies would have to win at West Point and without support of the Brigade.

But Navy, behind the backfield of Hal Hamberg and Hillis Hume, was too strong. The Middies lost only once that season, to Notre Dame, and won their first Lambert Trophy as the East's best football team.

While Hamberg and Hume were the running stars, the appearance of an Army plebe named Glenn Davis was noteworthy. Davis didn't do a whole lot in the 1943 game, but he and

Navy overpowered Army in 1943 winning 13-0.
Courtesy of the United States Military Academy

his backfield partner, Felix "Doc" Blanchard, would make an indelible mark on college football—and the Army-Navy rivalry—over the next three years.

"Mr. Inside" and "Mr. Outside"

Davis brought speed and elusiveness to the Army lineup, while Blanchard was a powerful force in the middle.

Davis was recruited by Blaik by mail, not an unusual occurrence in those days. A speedster at Bonita High School in LaVerne, California, Davis scored 256 points in his senior season. He won the Knute Rockne Trophy as southern California's top high school track athlete. So Blaik wrote a letter to Davis' parents, who were at first leery about sending their twin sons—Glenn's brother Ralph also drew interest from West Point—across the country during the war. There also was some question whether Glenn Davis could handle the academy's scholastic requirements, particularly with West Point classes graduating in three years during the war. Davis had to do some serious studying to pass the entrance exams.

And while he played as a freshman, he didn't last the entire academic year, leaving West Point in December after struggling with a math course. After bulking up on math at Pomona College in California, he returned the next year, even more determined to prove himself. "I had felt as if I had let many people down, and I was not going to allow that (to happen) again," Davis said. "I came back to West Point to stay at the academy and succeed."

During his return trip to the Hudson Valley, Davis met Clark Shaughnessy on the train ride east. Shaughnessy, one of the greatest coaches in football history, mentioned another player headed for West Point: Felix Blanchard.

While Davis was the speedster who couldn't be caught, Blanchard was the perfect complement: a punishing six-foot, 210-pounder (big for those days) who could run over tacklers and also eliminate them with crunching blocks.

Blanchard took his prep school team in Bay St. Louis, Mississippi, to an undefeated season in 1941, when he was a senior. The coaching staff at the Point actively recruited him.

"They had contacted me about going to West Point when I was in high school," said Blanchard, "but at that point in time I really wasn't interested. Academically, I never was too hot, so I never had any idea I would pass the entrance examination and go to West Point." So he enrolled at North Carolina for one year, but Blanchard was eager to serve in the war. He first attempted to enlist in the Navy, but did not pass the physical because of poor vision—ironic because, after his stint at West Point, Blanchard would become a pilot and flight instructor and once landed a burning plane in the English countryside, avoiding more populated areas and saving many lives.

Blanchard was allowed to enlist in the Army, but before he served, his father, known as "Big Doc" to Felix's "Little Doc," arranged for an appointment to the academy. Sadly, "Big Doc" died a short time later.

Blaik knew what he had immediately: the foundation for an unstoppable backfield on offense, plus two staunch defensive players. Two potential all-Americans. Two possible Heisman Trophy winners.

Already, Blaik was using the T-formation to make the offense more diversified. With such talent in the backfield, including quarterback Arnold Tucker, Blaik was certain the Cadets' attack would be daunting. For one, he considered Blanchard the best fullback prospect in the history of college football, a player who not only could be the No. 1 runner

Felix "Doc" Blanchard.
Courtesy of the United States Military Academy

thanks to his combination of power and quickness, but a fearsome blocker who unselfishly would accept that less-glamorous role for the good of the team.

"I don't think Doc Blanchard ever thought twice about who got the ball or who got the touchdowns," Blaik said. "As long as Army was scoring the touchdowns and winning the games, he was as big a part of the success as if he was the one in the end zone."

Indeed, Blaik once likened Blanchard to a decathlete—Blanchard was a shot putter at Army, as well, although it was Davis who made more of a reputation on the track.

Davis also was a fine baseball and basketball player, but for their three seasons together at West Point, they made headlines and won awards and national championships on the gridiron.

Glenn Davis.
Courtesy of the United States Military Academy

And it wasn't just their skills on offense that made Blanchard and Davis stand out. "Mr. Inside" was a fearsome tackler, while Davis could cover any opposing speedster.

By the time they appeared together in an Army-Navy game, Blanchard and Davis had led the Cadets to an unbeaten record. A victory over the Mids not only would snap the five-game slide in which Army had managed only six points and been blanked four times, but it would secure the first undefeated season since 1916 for the Black Knights.

The 1944 classic had one of the most unusual buildups in Army-Navy history. With the war going well on both fronts, and with the opportunity to augment the sale of war bonds through ticket purchases, the government moved the game site from Annapolis to Baltimore. Navy would remain the home team for the game at Municipal Stadium, which could hold nearly 70,000 fans; more than $58.6 million would be raised in bonds sales.

Blaik suspected Navy of doctoring the field. He was told the hosts were putting down a new turf field, but what he believed

Blaik looks on as the Army players toss their helmets into the air.
Courtesy of the United States Military Academy

the Middies were doing was providing a soft, mushy track to slow down the Cadets' awesome ground game.

While Blaik and his assistants would get nowhere in trying to halt the resodding, they would get exactly where they wanted on that new turf. But, first, they had to get to Baltimore, and it was no infantry maneuver they used.

Instead, a "training" mission was used to transport the Cadets to Baltimore. Two days before the game, the USS *Uruguay* set sail down the Hudson to the Chesapeake Bay, accompanied by camouflaged destroyers. The Cadets would learn about troop transit, antisubmarine warfare, and convoy procedures during the voyage to the game.

While the Corps was sequestered on the *Uruguay* when it arrived on the eve of the game, a band of sophomores, dressed in civilian clothing, sneaked off the ship and past dock security. These young gentlemen took a cab to Annapolis for one of the great raids in Army-Navy history. The Cadets painted "Beat Navy" on the famed statue of Tecumseh and placed a Cadets cap on Tecumseh's head.

Things wouldn't get any better for the Midshipmen on game day. After the Cadets marched from the *Uruguay* to the stadium, a distance estimated at five miles, they witnessed the first of three magnificent performances by Blanchard and Davis against Navy. Blaik's "storybook team" played inspired football, particularly on defense, against a Navy squad the Army coach said was "second to none, aside from us, of course." Bob Jenkins, Navy's star halfback, was injured early in the game on a hard tackle by one of Blaik's favorite players, Bobby Dodds. Not long after, another important Middie, Don Whitmire, hurt his ankle.

Not that a fully healthy Navy team would have beaten the Cadets this day. With so much incentive—an unbeaten season,

Earl Blaik (center) with Doc Blanchard and Glenn Davis.
Courtesy of the United States Military Academy

breaking the slide against their archrival, and a national championship—the Cadets were overwhelming.

Although Navy did draw within 9-7 in the third quarter, Davis ensured Army was not in any trouble. He intercepted a pass and then Blanchard went to work behind his formidable offensive line. Doc and his blockers wore down the Middies on a 52-yard drive to a 10-yard touchdown run by Blanchard.

Davis clinched it with a brilliant 52-yard run down the sideline, and how typical of their styles was that? Blanchard ate up the clock with a meticulous display of muscle on a 52-yard march to the end zone. Then Davis made like an antelope with a dash of the same distance for another score.

"Mr. Inside" and "Mr. Outside" indeed.

The 23-7 win prompted Gen. Douglas MacArthur's famed telegram to his protegé, Blaik: "THE GREATEST OF ALL ARMY TEAMS. STOP. WE HAVE STOPPED THE WAR TO

CELEBRATE YOUR MAGNIFICENT SUCCESS. MACAR-
THUR."

Army won its first national championship in 1944, going
9-0. Davis led the nation with twenty touchdowns and also
threw for two scores as the Powerhouse from the Point scored
a record seventy-four touchdowns. Opponents managed only
five touchdowns and four of them—including Notre Dame by
59-0—were shut out.

Irish coach Ed McKeever said after that shellacking that
he'd "seen Superman in the flesh. He wears number 35 on his
Army jersey and his name is Doc Blanchard." Blanchard had
nine touchdowns that year.

But it was Davis who finished second for the Heisman Trophy behind Ohio State quarterback Les Horvath.

Along with Blanchard and Davis, four other Cadets made
all-America teams: Barney Poole, Jack Green, Joe Stanowicz,
and Doug Kenna. Blaik paid tribute to them and their teammates with a souvenir book he sent to each player on the 1944
squad. Inside the book was a message from the coach:

"Seldom in a lifetime's experience is one permitted the complete satisfaction of being part of a perfect performance. To the
coaches, the 23-7 is enough. To the squad members: By hard
work and sacrifice, you superbly conditioned ability, ambition
and the desire to win, thereby leaving a rich athletic heritage
for future academy squads. From her sons West Point expects
the best—you were the best. In truth, you were a storybook
team."

And the story would get even better.

By the 1945 season, the Second World War was over and
MacArthur was calling for a "better world." Peace came at a
very expensive price in American lives, and the celebrations
that followed V-E and V-J days were tinged with sadness.

Nowhere was that more true than at the academies, where

many former Corps and Brigade members had given their lives to preserve freedom. Both the Cadets and Middies who played football understood that the best way to honor their fallen brethren was to excel at their specialty. In 1945, for the second straight year, no college football team could touch the United States Military Academy at West Point. Nor could any opponent slow down what now had become the most famous sports tandem in the land: Blanchard and Davis.

Army was so mighty in 1945 that Blanchard and Davis became part-timers. As the Cadets stormed through their first eight contests, including five shutouts and another mauling of Notre Dame (48-0), the backfield duo made the cover of *Time* magazine and was acclaimed from coast to coast. Each played only 56 percent of the snaps because of all the routs, but that was enough for Davis to have a phenomenal 944 yards on eighty-two carries, scoring fifteen times, while Blanchard had sixteen touchdowns and won the Heisman. Davis was the runner-up, and Blanchard said that, given a ballot, he would have voted for Davis.

Blanchard also was the first football player to win the Sullivan Award, given to the best amateur athlete in America.

Entering the Navy game, the Cadets were poised to win a second straight national crown with yet another unblemished season. They were favorites against the Middies, who owned a 7-0-1 mark and were the most dangerous opponent Army faced all year. In fact, a Navy victory probably would have earned the Midshipmen the championship.

As good as Navy was, however, it was overmatched by Blaik's bunch. And as if the Cadets needed more inspiration, they were addressed by telephone by Gen. Dwight Eisenhower before the game at a rally for the team. "It is just 31 years since I participated in a 'Beat Navy' meeting," Ike said with some self-deprecating wit. "That year I was a cheerleader. I'd like to ask this year's occupant of the same post whether he is any more successful than I was in impressing that gang with his eloquence or in dodging the bombardment of catcalls and insults that was always my portion. Luckily, I had a broken leg and the Corps was gentlemanly enough to abstain from physical violence against a cripple.

"Anyway, we licked Navy."

They did so again in 1945, 32-13, in front of President Truman and many leaders of the armed forces. A 20-0 lead settled the game after one quarter. Blanchard's two short runs and a 49-yard burst by Davis—"Mr. Outside" shot through the line off-tackle, Blanchard territory, for that score—put Navy in far too deep a hole to climb out of against these Cadets. Blanchard even had a 52-yard return of an interception to cap one of the finest performances of his stellar career.

Perhaps giddy from so much success, Blaik dubbed the 1945 squad his very best. He also wondered if it was the best in the history of the sport. With an opportunity to further stake such a claim by playing in the Rose Bowl, to which it was invited, Army turned down the trip to Pasadena.

"What more could be out there for this team?" Blaik said, although he later would grow to regret not accepting the bowl bid. There was, Blaik and the Cadets would discover, much more out there for the Army team. Such as another unbeaten season, perhaps? Another Heisman Trophy? Another national championship?

For Blanchard and Davis, there was a co-captaincy of the football squad and their final year at West Point. After his early academic problems, Davis had adjusted well to the military student life. But, unlike Blanchard, he never was a natural for it. "I was pretty emotional and wasn't always able to keep things inside," Davis said. "I worried about everything—except when I was on the field. Before the games, I would be really tense, and that's how I'd be in the classroom a lot of the time. I guess you could say football was a relief for me."

Facing "Mr. Outside" was no relief for any opponent. And Davis just piled it on in 1946. Davis was so effective in 1946 that he not only grabbed the Heisman, but was voted The AP's athlete of the year. Bill Yeoman, who went on to coach the University of Houston, once told the *Los Angeles Times*: "There are words to describe how good an athlete Doc Blanchard was. But there aren't any words to describe how good Davis was."

In 1946, Davis had to go it alone early in the season when Blanchard was sidelined with a knee injury suffered in the opener against Villanova. In the fourth game, Tucker went out with a separated shoulder, but Army kept on winning. The only blemish by the time the Cadets reached their annual match-up with the Midshipmen was a 0-0 tie against Notre Dame, which broke a string of twenty-five consecutive wins.

Navy had fallen on hard times, even with the return of Tom Hamilton as coach. The Mids, with injuries ravaging the roster, were 1-7 and huge underdogs against the Cadets, who with a blowout victory would almost certainly win a third consecutive national crown. No team had won three successive titles—nor has any school done so in the succeeding years of the AP poll.

This hardly was the first time one of the academies was in a down period and the other was dominant. But, as Hamilton told his players before the game in Philadelphia: "This is Army-Navy, gentlemen, and that means the records have no bearing. We're their equals, they are our equals."

Well, not quite. At least not when 28-point favorite Army broke to a 21-6 halftime lead. It appeared the Cadets would ease to a third straight win over Navy in Blanchard's and Davis' final game.

Each scored in the first half, with Blanchard still not completely healthy, looking more like Davis on a 52-yard scamper.

Davis even threw a touchdown pass to Blanchard after Yeoman's interception.

Then, Army collapsed. Perhaps worn out from three seasons of near perfection, of being front-page news in the sports sections and, sometimes, the news sections, the Cadets simply had no energy left. Hamilton's team sensed it, too. Navy scored early in the third quarter, then stopped Blanchard on a short fourth-down run—indisputable evidence that Army's tank was empty.

Two minutes into the final period, a 2-yard touchdown catch by Leon Bramlett made it 21-18. But for the third straight time, Navy missed the extra point.

So three botched conversions was all that separated the academies heading into the dying moments of the game. Army couldn't move the ball because quarterback Tucker was hobbled by a leg injury and couldn't drop back to throw. The Middies put nearly every defender at the line to stop Davis, who couldn't get outside, and Blanchard, who was stymied inside.

Nearly 100,000 fans—everyone outside of the Brigade and their family members—had expected Blanchard and Davis to crown their nonpareil careers with a rout of Navy. Instead, one of the biggest upsets in the series and perhaps all of college football appeared imminent.

"Everything was in their favor at that point," Blaik said. "Everything we had worked so hard for all year was in danger of falling apart. But, if nothing else, we were a courageous bunch. We were up against a courageous team, and we needed to show our courage."

Navy took over at its 33 for what would be the pivotal possession. Inexorably, the Middies drove downfield, to the Army 23. Fullback Lynn Chewning ate up twenty of those yards and, with the Brigade frenzied and the Corps stunned, the Middies prepared to finish up the surprise ending.

Fans had left the stands to line the field, adding even more suspense to the proceedings. Would they prematurely rush the field if Navy scored with time left on the clock? Would they somehow interfere with play?

Navy had no timeouts remaining after Chewning was stopped on two runs. Following a five-yard penalty, the Mids tried a pitch on a sweep, but Poole made a superb tackle at the 4. With Navy trying to get off another play and officials ruling Bill Hawkins, the ballcarrier, did not get out of bounds to stop the clock, the final seconds ticked off. Army held on, 21-18.

"The most exhausting finish I can ever remember," Davis said. And one of the most exhilarating.

The Blanchard-Davis era came to an end not with a thunderous stampede or swift soiree, but with a sigh of relief—and even some disappointment, because Notre Dame was voted national champions. "I guess the AP was just mad at us," Blanchard said. "We had been around so long, they were looking for something new."

Davis was enraged by the balloting. "My reaction is we were the national champions the year before and no one beat us," he said. "Like anything else, you have to beat the champion to be the champion."

Davis was the individual champion, of course, by winning the Heisman. He concluded his marvelous career with 4,129 yards and fifty-nine touchdowns. His 11.5 yards a carry in 1945 remains an NCAA record for Division I, as does his career 8.3-yard average per carry. "He was one of the best," former Army guard Joe Steffy said of Davis, who died in March 2005. "He left an impression. The first time I met him, I was in awe. What he meant to the Military Academy and the game needs no explanation."

Blanchard might have become the first player to win two Heismans had he not been slowed by injury in 1946. But he made his impact even when he was not 100 percent, and Blaik paid his stars tribute by saying, "Doc and Glenn did more for West Point football than any other player or coach in history." Both became lieutenants upon graduation, but before entering the Army, each was drafted by NFL teams. Detroit chose Davis and Pittsburgh selected Blanchard. Each was offered big money—$130,000 over three seasons—to play in the new All-America Football Conference, too.

That left them with difficult decisions. Blanchard and Davis were determined to honor their military commitments, but they each were enticed by a chance to play pro football. They sought a two-month furlough beyond the two months they automatically received when they graduated, which would have freed them to play together for the 49ers in the AAFC. While West Point Superintendent Maj. Gen. Maxwell Taylor approved the request, there was a public outcry about preferential treatment, and permission was not granted.

Although they appeared together in a film, *The Spirit of West Point*, they would never again play as a tandem. Davis tore up his leg during the filming and while he did join the infantry, the knee never was the same. He wound up in the NFL with the Rams for two seasons, but was a shadow of the "Mr. Outside" who could outrun the wind.

Blanchard entered the Air Force and had a productive, even heroic career, as his skill in avoiding disaster with that burning airplane displayed.

Blaik knew there could be a serious letdown at the Point once Blanchard and Davis moved on. It was a measure of his coaching genius that the Cadets didn't spiral downward the rest of the decade. Instead, they had only one "down year," going 5-2-2 in 1947, when Columbia ended the Cadets' thirty-two-game unbeaten streak over three-and-a half years with a 21-20 verdict. But Army beat Navy again, 21-0.

By 1948, the Cadets again were poised to win a national crown. They were 8-0 entering the finale, and the Middies were 0-8, with three losses to undefeated teams. Navy had fallen thirteen straight times.

Still, if everyone associated with the Army-Navy game hadn't learned it two years earlier, records are no measurement of what the Cadets and Middies have in store for one another.

President Truman, who was a regular at the classic, again was on hand for what Blaik would call "a game that rivaled the great 21-21 tie of 1926 for excitement and level of performance." By then, two-platoon football had become the rage, although ironman stints still were common at the academies. What the Cadets really needed, though, were cast-iron stomachs, because much of the squad was ravaged by food poisoning two days before the contest. Perhaps that was a great equalizer, but Navy held Army to a 14-14 tie through three periods. It was difficult to tell which team had won all those games and which was winless.

Army quarterback Arnold Galiffa scored on a 10-yard run on the first play of the fourth quarter to bring a semblance of sanity back to the scoreboard. But Navy had its own star in Bill Hawkins, the guiding force of a long, drive deep into Army territory. Would the Middies again run out of time as they threatened an upset? Or would they find the end zone and produce at least a tie? Three times, the Cadets stood firm defensively, making memories of 1946 well up in everyone. "For any of us at Annapolis who witnessed the 1946 game, to be denied again would have been crushing," Hawkins said. "Our determination could not be measured."

On fourth down, Hawkins surged behind his line for three yards and a touchdown. When Roger Drew made the extra point, it was 21-21.

The Cadets still had time to spoil Navy's day, but Hawkins broke up a pass to thwart Army's attempt to come back.

If ever a tie felt like a win, especially after four successive losses, this one was sweet for the Middies. It also provided a superb climax to a historic decade in America's greatest sports rivalry.

8

UPSETS AND UPHEAVALS, 1950-1959

The Korean War was just beginning, the Cold War was heating up, and the Soviet Union and United States were blasting off in the space race. With so much happening at such a furious pace in the 1950s, it was hard to keep up. The world was changing, and so were the fortunes of the Army and Navy football teams.

After dominating Navy and just about everyone else from the Blanchard-Davis era right up to the end of the 1940s, Army had a sudden comeuppance in 1950. And then the Cadets would soon be embarrassed by a scandal that not only cost the football team, but undermined the very character of the academy itself.

The 1950 meeting between Army and Navy followed a recent pattern in the series—the Cadets came into the game with an 8-0 record, while Navy had won only two of eight games.

Navy had no chance against Army. At least that's what the "wise guys" figured. But, as usual in Army-Navy games, nothing could be left to logic. Somehow, Navy managed to pull off a 14-2 victory and hand the Cadets their first loss in twenty-nine games. Eddie Erdelatz, the new Navy coach, called it "the greatest team effort I've ever seen."

Army coach Earl Blaik, meanwhile, was pretty much at a loss for words. "They out-charged us," Blaik said. Trying to analyze a loss was genuinely foreign to Blaik. After all, it was only his third defeat in seven seasons (57-3-4).

Analyzing what happened the following year was almost impossible.

In 1951, ninety cadets, including thirty-seven football players, were dismissed from the academy in a scandal involving their cheating on exams. Blaik was so distraught he considered resigning. But he continued on at the request of Gen. Douglas MacArthur, who himself would be relieved of command in Korea in another shocking development.

The 1951 season was predictable for a decimated Army team: a 2-7 record, including a 42-7 loss to Navy, the highest *winning* score to that juncture by a team in the rivalry. It was, incidentally, also the first time both teams entered the game with losing records, and the first time the Army-Navy game was shown live on television.

It didn't take long for Blaik to turn things around. This set the stage for two more of the series' greatest games.

In 1954 Army was battling Navy for Lambert Trophy honors as the best team in the East. It was Army's top offensive team in the country against Navy's top defensive team and No. 2 offense. Guided by quarterback George Welsh, later to become *the most* successful Navy coach, the Middies' "Team Named Desire" clinched a Sugar Bowl berth with a 27-20 win over Army. Navy's defense was the star of the game, stopping the Cadets in the late going on the Middies' 8-yard line.

In 1955, Blaik was in desperate need of a quarterback. He

took a chance by moving all-American end Don Holleder to the position. A dumb move, it was generally thought. After all, Holleder had never played the position before. And he was giving up an almost certain second all-American honor at end by doing so.

SACRIFICE

Don Holleder could have been one of the greatest ends in Army football history. He helped Army lead the nation in total offense in 1954, when the Cadets were 7-2, but lost to Navy 27-20.

Red Blaik had other ideas. In desperate need of a star in his backfield after graduations, injuries and disciplinary measures hit the roster hard, Blaik turned to his all-American receiver.

Holleder was stunned, even asking Blaik if he could "sleep on it" before deciding whether to accept Blaik's suggestion of moving to quarterback.

Of course, Holleder knew it was his duty to obey a commanding officer. And while the coach had not exactly ordered Holleder to make the switch, the suggestion was not something a West Point cadet refused.

"I can't say I was comfortable with the idea when he first brought it up," Holleder said. "It was more a shock. But he felt I could do the job, so I was willing to do it."

The switch of Holleder to quarterback was a gamble by Blaik, who knew he was weakening one position and perhaps not strengthening another. Then again, Blaik was certain Holleder had the athletic skills, strength, speed, and intelligence to be the quarterback. And he knew Holleder had the leadership skills.

Still, with Holleder behind center, Army wouldn't be much of a passing threat. And when Holleder broke his ankle in spring practice, Blaik took some heavy criticism, with the move being dubbed "Blaik's Folly."

Not one to back down, Blaik wouldn't doubt his decision—or Holleder's abilities—even after losses to Syracuse (with Jim Brown) and Michigan in which Army scored a total of two points. Confronted by the West Point superintendent about the quarterbacking situation, Blaik steadfastly defended Holleder, and suggested the superintendent do so publicly, as well.

With such a vote of confidence, Holleder and Army turned their season around and was 5-3 when it met a strong Navy team that was 6-1-1 and heavily favored with George Welsh, the nation's leading passer, guiding the offense.

Blaik's pregame speech was more a plea to his players not to force him to walk across the Municipal Stadium field to congratulate Navy coach Eddie Erdelatz on his team's win. Holleder vowed: "Colonel, you are not going to have to take that walk."

After Navy's first drive covered seventy-six yards to a touchdown, the Cadets were able to shut down the Middies, with Holleder contributing strongly on defense. And late in the half, he took the Cadets to the Navy 1, but ran out of time.

Holleder made sure the Cadets weren't denied on their next possession, driving them forty-one yards to a touchdown and the lead, 7-6. All of the yards were gained on the ground. Indeed, Army had 283 yards total offense, none of it through the air. But Holleder brought the Cadets home a winner, prompting Army's best-known football fan, Gen. Douglas MacArthur, to fire off a telegram to Blaik and Holleder:

No victory the Army has won in its long years of fierce football struggles has ever reflected a greater spirit of raw courage, of invincible determination, of masterful strategic planning and resolute practical execution. To come from behind in the face of apparent insuperable odds is the true stamp of a champion. You and your tremendous team have restored faith and brought joy and gratification to millions of loyal Army fans.

His football career over—he would be inducted into the National Football Foundation Hall of Fame in 1985—Holleder went to infantry and paratroopers school. He worked his way up to major and was posted to Vietnam. On October 17, 1967, at the battle of Ong Thanh, Holleder was flying his helicopter over a battle area when he saw wounded American soldiers attempting to escape an ambush. He landed and, while trying to reach those soldiers, was shot and killed.

"He was a risk-taker who put the common good ahead of himself, whether it was giving up a position in which he had excelled or putting himself in harm's way in an attempt to save the lives of his men," said Michael Robert Patterson in his eulogy of Holleder. "In a day when acts of heroism were the rule rather than the exception, his stood out."

Jim Shelton, a member of Holleder's battalion, played football against Holleder while Shelton was at Delaware. When he saw the fallen Holleder, Shelton said, "I couldn't believe that he could be dead, how a guy as powerful and full of strength could be so lifeless. It was a very sad day, and unforgettable."

Each year, Shelton and some friends would journey to West Point and visit the Holleder Center, which houses the basketball and hockey facilities at the academy. A plaque honoring Holleder hangs in the lobby, along with a painting of him in combat uniform, wearing a belt of hand grenades and carrying a rifle. A memorial from the Black Lions, the 228th Infantry Battalion whose wounded men Holleder tried to rescue, sits in a trophy case. Shelton called it "a wonderful tribute to a hero."

Holleder is buried in Arlington National Cemetery, and the name Donald E. Holleder can be found on panel 28E, row 25 of the Vietnam Veterans Memorial Wall in Washington, D.C.

The move was highly criticized. Some called it "Blaik's Folly," particularly after a 26-2 loss to Michigan and a 13-0 defeat by Syracuse. Blaik was undaunted. He continued to use Holleder, and the converted quarterback continued to improve. At the end of the season, Blaik's reputation was restored when Holleder led Army over Navy 14-6 despite another great performance by Welsh.

Blaik was just full of surprises. Later in the 1950s he came up with the "Lonely End" formation, which caught opponents by surprise and quickly caught the attention of the nation. When Army lined up for a play in 1958, there was Bill Carpenter split wide from the formation on the line—in effect, a split end. Nor did he return to the huddle after the play. He had been instructed not to return so he could conserve time and energy he usually lost running back and forth after each play. The Army quarterback would communicate with the six-foot-two, 210-pound Carpenter by sign language. Meanwhile, Blaik's purpose for the "Lonely End" was to spread the field and improve the Cadets' passing game. And with Carpenter excused from the huddle, the Cadets would be able to get plays off faster.

Opposing teams were soon scrambling to cover this strange new formation that featured the beginnings of the modern-day wide receiver. Not only was Army's passing game improved, but the formation opened holes for Pete Dawkins to run through. It was a big reason why Dawkins was able to win the Heisman Trophy that year.

In 1958, Carpenter caught twenty-two passes for 453 yards and two touchdowns. In 1959, Carpenter succeeded Dawkins as an all-American. That season, he had forty-three receptions for 591 yards and four touchdowns.

Carpenter was drafted by pro football teams from both the NFL and AFL, but decided to become a career military officer. During the Vietnam War, he won presidential acclaim for his

Three Heisman Trophy winners: Glenn Davis, Doc Blanchard,
and Pete Dawkins.
Courtesy of the United States Military Academy

heroism when he ordered an air strike on his own position in an attempt to save what remained of his unit.

Army's 22-6 win over Navy in 1958 completed an 8-0-1 record for the Cadets and also finished an era at West Point.

It was the last season at Army for Blaik, who went out on top after an agonizing start to the decade. He handed the coaching reins to Dale Hall, a former reserve Army halfback who played on the Blanchard-Davis teams.

Erdelatz, who had a 5-3-1 record against Army as the Navy coach, also decided to leave his post. He left his successor, Wayne Hardin, in pretty good shape.

One of the players coming into his own at Navy was running back Joe Bellino. And just around the corner would be another great one, a fellow by the name of Roger Staubach.

SOLDIER OF GOOD FORTUNE

When "Lonesome End" Bill Carpenter replaced Pete Dawkins as captain of the Army football team in 1959, so the story goes, he was seen taking off his shoes at a West Point reservoir.

Asked what he was doing, Carpenter replied: "They want me to follow in Pete Dawkins' footsteps. I have to learn to walk on water."

No, Dawkins never walked on water. But he did just about everything else in a masterful athletic and academic career at West Point.

He won the Heisman Trophy in 1958 as a triple-threat halfback who could run, throw, and catch passes. He also starred on the Army hockey team and played baseball.

Off the field, he was president of his class and ranked in the top 5 percent, and also was first captain of cadets. Somehow, he found time to sing in the West Point choir and play several musical instruments.

"I was, uh, sort of intense," Dawkins said.

His life after West Point was also "sort of intense." He was a Rhodes Scholar and went to England to study and play rugby for Oxford University. While doing so, he merely revolutionized the game with a different type of passing technique on scrum throw-ins.

A few other highlights of his varied accomplishments:

He served in Korea and Vietnam and became the Army's youngest general at forty-five.
He earned a Ph.D. with two postgraduate degrees at Princeton.
He became a White House fellow and ran for the United States Senate.
He became a financial chief on Wall Street.

As well as being a masterful athlete on the football field,
Pete Dawkins starred on the Army hockey team.
Courtesy of the United States Military Academy

Sort of intense, indeed.

And guess which accomplishment keeps popping up in Dawkins' life? That's right, the Heisman Trophy.

"It's humbling and astounding to me that all over the world when people find out you're a Heisman winner, they immediately identify with it," he says. "It epitomizes what college football is all about."

When Dawkins was a young boy in Bloomfield,

Michigan, no one would have given him a chance to do anything special as an athlete. His growth was stunted by polio and he was labeled "Squirt" by mean-spirited kids.

As a freshman in high school, Dawkins weighed only ninety-seven pounds and was the smallest player on his team. That's when he started bodybuilding on his own—long before it became fashionable in team sports.

"Every night, I repeatedly lifted five-pound coffee cans filled with cement," he said.

When he got to West Point at the age of seventeen, Dawkins was still lifting weights even though it was against academy rules. He would hide the barbell under his bed and lift after lights were out.

The onetime ninety-seven-pounder was now six foot one and weighed close to two hundred pounds. Dawkins had his heart set on quarterback, but was thrown for a loss when dropped from the team by Earl Blaik. Seeing that Dawkins was bitterly disappointed, the Army coach suggested he might try out as a running back.

First, though, he had to show his mettle in returning punts in practice. It was hellish for Dawkins, who kept getting pounded and pushed around by Army's big special-teams defenders.

He worked hard and eventually turned things around for himself.

"Finally, I ran one back all the way, then another and the coaches agreed: 'Maybe he could be a running back,'" Dawkins remembered many years later.

A running back, indeed. And one who could pass left-handed while on the run, and haul in passes with exceptional hands. Oh, yes, Dawkins also returned kickoffs and ran back punts.

Dawkins started out the 1958 season impressively, scoring four touchdowns—two by rushing and two on receptions—in a 45-8 victory over South Carolina.

"He was a tremendous runner, a beautiful faker in changing directions as he gained 113 yards in nine rushes, and an equally vivid pass receiver," reported the *New York Times*.

Against Penn State, Dawkins scored on a 6-yard run and 72-yard pass play to lead Army's 26-0 victory over the Nittany Lions.

In the season's third game, Dawkins scored the clinching touchdown on a 6-yard run with seven seconds remaining as Army beat Notre Dame 14-2.

After three games, Dawkins had rushed for 261 yards, an average of 6.9 yards, and received the ultimate praise from Blaik.

"This boy is a born leader," Blaik said. "He is only twenty, yet very mature. He has given us inspiration and direction. I trust him with more responsibilities than probably any captain I've had in the past."

Dawkins said his game was lifted by Blaik's new "Lonely End" offense. It featured a formation placing end Carpenter on the flank, some fifteen to eighteen yards from the tackle, and opened up running and receiving lanes for Dawkins and others.

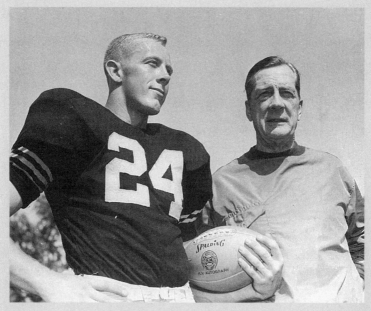

Pete Dawkins with Earl Blaik.
Courtesy of the United States Military Academy

"This 'Lonely End' offense is the thing that has given us spark, brought us alive," Dawkins said. "With the espirit de corps this gang has, any captain would look good."

A leg injury forced Dawkins out of Army's 35-6 rout of Virginia early in the second half. Dawkins then missed the Pitt game, a 14-14 tie.

Dawkins returned for Game 6 against Colgate, highlighting a 68-6 victory with a 75-yard touchdown catch. In addition, he scored the two-point conversion on a run and also passed for another two-pointer after an Army score.

Against Rice, Dawkins caught a 64-yard touchdown pass with fifty-two seconds left for the decisive score as Army won, 14-7. Dawkins then scored three touchdowns to lead Army past Villanova 26-0 in his final game at Michie Stadium.

Then came Navy. Playing his least productive game of the year statistically, Dawkins didn't score a touchdown or throw a touchdown pass in the finale. His only contribution on the scoreboard was a two-point conversion pass to Bob Anderson for the final score in Army's 22-6 victory. It was a sweet win for Dawkins and the Cadets, who had lost to Navy 14-0 in 1957. The halfback called it his "biggest thrill."

By then, the nation's sportswriters were pretty much convinced Dawkins was the best college football player in the country.

Dawkins, who had earlier been selected to the all-American team and won the Maxwell Trophy as the top player, took the Heisman in a landslide. Dawkins outpointed his closest competitor, Iowa's Randy Duncan, 1,394 to 1,021.

Dawkins became the third West Pointer to win the Heisman, following Doc Blanchard and Glenn Davis. The voters had to be impressed with Dawkins' versatility, a combination of "Mr. Inside and Mr. Outside."

Dawkins rushed for 428 yards on only seventy-eight carries and caught sixteen passes for 491 yards, totaling twelve touchdowns. In addition, he returned seven kickoffs for 132 yards and ran back ten punts for 162 yards.

In Dawkins' mind, the statistics were overshadowed by the Navy game.

"Two memories from my last Army-Navy game in 1958 really stand out, and to this day I wish I could make the first one go away," Dawkins said.

That would be when he fumbled the opening kickoff.

The other memory was much better for him.

"I was standing on the field at the end of the game, singing the alma mater and being struck very poignantly by how special it was to have the opportunity to be a part of this game," Dawkins said.

Another important memory for Dawkins: the time Gen. Douglas MacArthur visited West Point to talk to the football team.

MacArthur told the Cadets: "You're not just playing for the academy. You're playing for the ghosts of a million American soldiers who fought and died for their country, and are now looking down on you. Now go out and win!"

MacArthur's fiery speech made a big impact on Dawkins, who thought about it whenever he went out to face an opponent.

He was equally inspired by something else—fear.

"It's not a fear of losing or a fear of putting up bad statistics," he said. "It's a fear of letting down the Corps of Cadets and a fear of letting down the tradition of the Army team."

9

NAVY'S HEISMAN HEROES, 1960-1969

In 1957 *Washington Post* reporter Martie Zap was approached by an excited Edgar "Rip" Miller, the former Middies coach.

"He was really enthused," Zap later recalled. "He wanted me to come over to Plebe Field and look at somebody. That was the first time I saw Joe Bellino, and you could tell just watching him that he was somebody special."

Special, indeed.

By 1960, Bellino became the first at Navy to win the coveted Heisman Trophy as the best college football player in the country.

A couple of years later, the Middies had another player who was also pretty special—Roger Staubach. By 1963, Staubach won the Heisman as well.

Within a period of just four seasons, the two players became inextricably linked as winners of college football's most prestigious award.

Two Heisman Trophy winners—Navy's only two Heisman winners—with two different styles.

In his Navy career as a standout quarterback, Staubach was low-key and careful not to make any comments that might be considered controversial or boastful.

Bellino wasn't quite so reticent.

"I figure I've got at least one 50-yard run in me in every game," the five-foot-nine, 180-pound Bellino unabashedly told the media.

Very often, he was right, give or take a few yards.

Against Army in 1959 he ripped off a 47-yard touchdown run, one of three he made against the Cadets that day in a 43-12 Navy rout—the highest score to that point by either team in the rivalry. On a shorter scoring run that day, Bellino showed why he was such a creative runner.

The play was designed for Bellino to go over right tackle and cut to the middle. But once he found a gaping hole on the right side, he simply swung over to the right sidelines and scored on a 15-yard dash.

"I was supposed to cut to the middle," Bellino explained, "but it's easier to go outside—especially when there's no one there."

Bellino insisted he was an obedient player, "like any good Midshipman should be." But that didn't mean he would always follow orders on a football field.

Wayne Hardin, who coached both Bellino and Staubach, once remembered:

"Against Maryland (in 1959), it was late in the fourth quarter, we had used all of our timeouts and were behind by five points. They had to punt from their 10-yard line and I yelled to Bellino to run out of bounds after he caught the punt so we could stop the clock.

"He took the kick and I'm yelling, 'run out of bounds, run

Joe Bellino.
Courtesy of the United States Naval Academy

out of bounds.' Well, I watched him run all the way into the end zone for a touchdown and then over the bounds marker. When he got back to the bench, he said, 'I ran out of bounds down there just like you told me to.'"

Playing for Navy had always been a dream of Bellino's.

"I could have gone to West Point," Bellino said. "They promised me an appointment. But since I was a junior in high school (in Winchester, Massachusetts), I wanted to go to Navy."

Bellino always seemed to have some kind of interesting story associated with his runs, adding to his storied college career. Try one particular 50-yard touchdown dash he made against Boston College in 1959.

As he crossed the goal line, Bellino began limping and suddenly fell down as if he had been shot.

Turns out the Middies were wearing knee-length socks that day for the first time. Because Bellino had extremely thick calves, the elastic rims on top of the socks had actually cut off circulation in his legs and turned his feet blue. The socks were cut, allowing Bellino to continue playing, and the Naval Academy ordered a different kind for Bellino's tree-trunk legs for the next game.

Bellino, also a star baseball player, had solid football seasons in 1958 and 1959. In 1960, the Massachusetts native outdid himself, and did it all for Navy as he led the Middies to a 9-1 regular-season record. Even a loss to Missouri in the Orange Bowl could not diminish the extraordinary year that Bellino had for Navy:

He rushed for 834 yards, more than half his team's total, scored eighteen touchdowns, threw two touchdown passes, caught seventeen passes for 280 yards, returned thirteen kick-offs for 206 yards and five punts for 97. He even kicked an extra point and when he wasn't on offense, he played some safety.

One of his biggest plays on defense came in the 1960 Army game, when Bellino intercepted a pass and returned it fifty yards to preserve a 17-12 victory.

After the game, an excited Navy publicist raced up to Bellino and proclaimed, "That play won you the Heisman Trophy!"

"Who are you kidding?" Bellino responded. "That play saved me from being a goat."

Bellino would later explain to a reporter:

"I had fumbled at the 30 and they were going in for the winning touchdown."

A couple of days after the game, Bellino was in class when he was called into the office of the academy superintendent. Bellino was concerned that it had to do with his schoolwork. Instead, the superintendent stood up and read a telegraph from the Downtown Athletic Club in New York that Bellino had won the Heisman Trophy.

"My first reaction was, 'Thank God it wasn't something to do with school,'" Bellino remembered several years later. "Then it hit me. I had won the top award in college football. I was taken aback."

Then along came Staubach.

One national magazine described the six-foot-two quarterback as "a truly dazzling athlete. He throws on the run, or backing up. Trapped, he has a startling quickness and a mysterious sense of the profitable direction."

Translation: With his dangerous scrambling ability, Staubach had more escape tricks than Houdini.

Staubach came of age at the end of his sophomore season in 1962 when he directed Navy's 34-14 rout of Army.

"I don't think I've ever been any more nervous before a game," Staubach recalled. "I don't know that I slept the whole night. (President and Navy man) John F. Kennedy was at the game, with 102,000 other people."

Staubach was a product of Cincinnati's strong Catholic Youth Organization and his mother couldn't remember a time he wasn't involved in organized sports.

President Kennedy among the crowd at the Army-Navy football game in 1962.
CORBIS

"From the time he was able to sit up, he was an active child," she said.

Staubach attended prep school at New Mexico Military Institute for a year before going to Annapolis. He was well aware of the Army-Navy football tradition.

"I had watched the previous games, of course, and saw Army guys like Pete Dawkins," Staubach said. "But once you're there with the brigade of Midshipmen, you really get caught up in it.

"On my first day at the Naval Academy, after they shaved off most of my hair, we all got a message from the superintendent where we all learned how to say, 'Beat Army.'"

That's just what Staubach did in two of the three times he faced the Cadets.

"Those games were as important emotionally to me as any games I've played in," said Staubach, who later won two Super Bowls with the Dallas Cowboys in a memorable pro football career.

Emotions were never higher than in the Army-Navy game of 1963. The contest had been postponed once because of the assassination of President Kennedy. When it was finally played on December 7, Navy held on by a 21-15 score in one of the series' all-time thrillers.

Army was driving for the winning score when time ran out on the Cadets with the ball sitting on Navy's 2-yard-line.

"That would've ruined our season," Staubach said of a loss to the Cadets. "We had beaten Michigan and Notre Dame, teams that were ranked, but winning the Army-Navy game made all the difference to us."

As Staubach emerged as the glamour player of college football in 1963, the Middies did a cover-up of their cover boy. They banned most interviews with their star player because they felt he might be overwhelmed. Postgame news conferences were closely monitored by the Middies' public relations staff and kept to a minimum.

Once, after Navy's dramatic 38-25 victory at Duke in 1963, the media waited for an hour to talk to "Rog," as he was called

Roger Staubach.
Courtesy of the United States Naval Academy

by the public relations staff. When he was finally produced to meet the press, Staubach appeared in his Navy blues with his white cap tucked under one arm. A bus with forty-three teammates sat idling in the parking lot, waiting to leave. When a photographer moved within three feet of Staubach to take his picture, he was stopped by a hand from one of the PR staff and admonished like a miscreant child. "Too close," the photographer was told.

Staubach kept his answers to reporters' questions short and riddled with clichés. The session lasted just eight minutes before Staubach was told to board the bus. When Staubach stopped to sign autographs for a group of teenagers, Hardin led interference.

"Write the academy, boys," Hardin told the teenagers. "He'll send you an autographed picture."

Hardin explained his thinking to a national magazine:

"More people would like to see Roger Staubach right now more than any celebrity. If we opened the doors, do you have any idea how many writers and photographers would show up at our practices? A dozen? It would be closer to 5,000."

There were times when it seemed that not even that many tacklers could handle the slippery Staubach, who deservedly earned the nickname, "Roger the Dodger."

Staubach was perfect for Hardin's football philosophy: plenty of razzle-dazzle and wide-open play.

In 1963, polished after a 5-5 sophomore season, he led the Middies to a 9-1 record, No. 2 ranking in the country, and a berth in a postseason bowl. Staubach became the first Navy quarterback to rush for more than one hundred yards in a game. At one point, Staubach set twenty-eight Navy records.

And even in a loss to top-ranked Texas in the Cotton Bowl, he was still breaking records with twenty-one of thirty-one pass completions and 228 yards in the Dallas classic.

Action on the field during the first quarter of the 1963 game.
Bettmann/CORBIS

After hitting the heights in 1963, Staubach was hampered by injuries in 1964 as Navy slumped to a 3-8-1 record, including an 11-8 loss to Army.

With the Staubach era behind them, the Middies were no longer the East's elite team. While Staubach was fulfilling his four-year service obligation that included a tour in Vietnam and then starting a brilliant NFL career at the age of twenty-seven, Navy football was sliding. The Middies crashed and burned in the latter part of the 1960s with 2-8 and 1-9 records, respectively, in 1968 and 1969.

Perhaps even more important to Navy: the Middies could only beat Army once in six tries from 1964–1969.

"Thank God we won some Army-Navy games when I played," Staubach said.

He said the losses during his Navy career were important, though: "I know what it's like to win big games and also to lose them. How to handle a loss prepares you for life, too."

CAN WE SEE THAT AGAIN?

The Army-Navy game should be historic. In 1963, it helped change television sports forever.

Thanks greatly to a former cadet, Tony Verna, instant replay was born during Navy's 21-15 victory.

On their way to Municipal Stadium on December 7—not only was it exactly twenty-two years after the Japanese bombed Pearl Harbor, but the game had been postponed one week after President Kennedy was assassinated—Verna told his CBS crew about his plans.

At some point in the telecast, he was going to unveil a replay of the previous play. Verna had been working on the idea since the 1960 Olympics.

"The idea came to me out of frustration," Verna said. "Before replays, football telecasts were filled with dead spots. You spent a lot of time watching receivers walk back to the huddle after incomplete passes. It really destroyed the momentum of the telecast.

"Replays gave you something to show during the pauses. It seemed to make the game go faster."

First, though, Verna had to sell CBS executives on the idea. Because he was one of the network's top directors, he got the go-ahead—with a few warnings.

Verna's boss, Bill McPhail, told him any problems during the most popular football event on television in 1963 would be like "messing up Cardinal Spellman's funeral." And McPhail insisted Verna make sure his announcers were comfortable with it.

Comfortable with it? When Verna told legendary play-by-play man Lindsey Nelson and his analyst, Terry Brennan, what he had planned, Nelson responded in a near-shriek: "You're going to do what?"

He was going to make history.

Verna's plan was to use a play featuring Navy star quarterback Roger Staubach, the Heisman Trophy winner. Unfortunately, no plays by Staubach stood out.

Plus, Verna was struggling with the videotape machine being used for the replay. In fact, he was forced to borrow an old tape of an *I Love Lucy* show for the replay—a tape he was forced to return, meaning the first sports video replay was not saved.

By the fourth quarter, Verna began to fear his groundbreaking idea would never reach the viewers. The technology was not cooperating.

"For most of the game it didn't work," Verna said. "Then late in the game, I heard the beeps straightening out, and I said, 'Stand by, Lindsey,' and I hear the picture straightening out and I say, 'Go, Lindsey.'"

The chosen play was not of Staubach but of his Army counterpart, Rollie Stichweh. When Stichweh broke a tackle and scored on a 1-yard run, the replay was queued up.

"*This is not live*," Nelson told the millions of television viewers. "Ladies and gentlemen, Army did not score again!"

Nor would it score again. And the video replay was not used any more that day, even as Stichweh led Army to the Navy 2-yard line before time ran out.

Verna, however, had taken the first revolutionary step. And he knew it.

"I think it's hard to imagine viewing sports without the instant replay," Verna said. "After that, every sporting event had to use it or people would complain."

Verna soon received a call from Dallas Cowboys general manager Tex Schramm, a former sports director at CBS who hired Verna at the network.

"My boy, what you have done here will have such far-reaching implications," Schramm said, "we can't begin to imagine them today."

10

MEDIOCRE TEAMS, MEMORABLE
GAMES, 1970-1979

It was shortly before the 1971 Army-Navy game in Philadelphia. There was a buzz around JFK Stadium that President Nixon would be attending.

A surge of excitement went through the huge crowd when a black limousine bearing commander-in-chief flags came through a gate at one end of the field. Tightly surrounded by what appeared to be secret service agents, the vehicle slowly encircled the cavernous old brick stadium until coming to a halt in front of the section occupied by cadets from the United States Military Academy.

The entire Corps stood up, snapped to attention and saluted smartly.

When the door to the limousine opened, out stepped . . . Bill XVII, the Navy goat. *Gotcha . . .*

The Middies roared with delight over the joke. In their

continuing game of one-upmanship, they had really put one over this time on the Cadets.

The chagrined Cadets got their revenge. They put one over on Navy themselves, topping the Middies 24-23 in a down-to-the-wire thriller.

Usually the games between the two weren't that close in the 1970s. Navy was normally beating Army by such lopsided scores as 51-0 in 1973, 19-0 in 1974, 30-6 in 1975, 38-10 in 1976, and 31-7 in 1979, the last year the game was played at JFK Stadium.

The night before the 1979 game, Navy coach George Welsh took his running backs out for a pregame walk around the old stadium. He kiddingly suggested they would have a big day against a thoroughly outmanned Army team. "I remember walking around the field with George and a bunch of players including Duane Flowers knowing that this was going to be the last Army-Navy game being played at that field," said Navy back Eddie Meyers. "I remember George coming up to me and saying, 'We got a fast track.' I was just smiling, grinning from ear to ear, 'Yep,' I said, 'Good things are going to happen.'"

They certainly did for Meyers. The next day, the sophomore gained a team-record 278 yards and scored three touchdowns for the Middies. He later topped his own mark with 298 yards against Syracuse in 1981.

These were tough times for the Army football program.

In 1970 Army struggled through its worst season to date at 1-9-1 and then went winless in ten games in 1973. Coach Tom Cahill was replaced by Homer Smith, who was replaced by Lou Saban, all within a six-year period.

One of the few bright spots for Army was quarterback Leamon Hall, who played from 1974–1977 and established career passing records that still stand at West Point.

Army's record for the 1970s was a distressing 36-68-3.

Navy, meanwhile, could at least boast of attending a post-season bowl game in the decade. That was 1978 when the Middies beat BYU 23-16 in the Holiday Bowl to cap a 9-3 season under Welsh, the second Navy coach of the decade after Rick Forzano.

And the Middies could at least boast of one first-team all-American, defensive back Chet Moeller in 1975.

Not that the Middies exactly tore apart the football landscape—their record in the decade was 49-62—but they did, after all, manage to beat Army in seven of ten meetings.

The few times Army came out on top, it was usually a close encounter of the nerve-wracking kind.

The 1971 game, for instance.

The faux presidential vehicle wasn't the only trick the Middies pulled on the Cadets that day. Before the game, they set a papier-mâché Army mule on fire and the Philadelphia Fire Department roared in to put out the blaze. The Army football team was just as hot at the start, rolling up a 16-0 lead after one quarter on a field goal by Jim Barclay and two touchdowns by Bob Hines. Then Navy started setting off some sparks of its own. Quarterback Fred Stuvek ran for two touchdowns in the second quarter and threw a 12-yard touchdown pass to Steve Ogden in the third to give the Middies a 21-16 lead.

It was far from over.

In the fourth quarter, Army quarterback Kingsley Fink tossed a 5-yard touchdown pass to Ed Francis, then completed another to John Simac for a two-point conversion, giving Army a 24-21 lead with 10:11 left in the game.

After the ensuing kickoff, a determined Navy team drove fifty yards in seven-and-a-half minutes to the Army 8-yard line. But on third down, Army's Steve Bogasian sacked Stuvek for a 12-yard loss and then Randy Stein intercepted the quarterback's pass on the next play.

Not over yet, folks.

Greg McGuckin fumbled on Army's first play from scrimmage, giving Navy the ball on the Cadets' 41 with 2:22 left. The Middies knifed quickly deep into Army territory. With the ball on the 7, Stuvek lateraled to George Berry and the runner swept down to the 1-yard line. But an official called the play back, saying that Stuvek's knee had touched the ground before he pitched the ball.

"I couldn't believe it," Stuvek said. "I was speechless."

The Middies now had the ball back on the Army 7.

Fourth down.

One play left.

A field goal to tie it?

Not on your life.

"In no way were we going for a field goal at the end," said Navy coach Forzano. "We aren't a tying team."

The play called was a pass from Stuvek to Andy Pease, but the ball trickled off the receiver's hands. The Cadets took over and allowed a Navy safety as they ran out the clock for the first one-point margin of victory in the rivalry's history.

The 1977 game was another of those nail-biters.

Like 1971, a Navy coach eschewed a chip-shot field goal that could have tied the game and went for the victory instead. With one minute to play, the Middies trailed 17-14, but had the ball on Army's 8-yard line. The Middies had one play left. A field goal would have tied it, and Navy coach Welsh had just the man to do it: Bob Tata, the nation's top field goal kicker.

Welsh instead called for an option pass by halfback Joe Gattuso Jr. The pass sailed over the straining, outstretched hands of receiver Phil McConkey, preserving Army's first win over Navy since 1972.

Welsh was questioned about the call after the game. His response:

"Army-Navy games are played to win or lose, not tie."

Indeed. One need only look at the record. In the first 105 games of the rivalry, the teams had only tied seven times.

The Army-Navy games of the 1970s were played against a backdrop of deeply disturbing news around the world:

At the start of the 1970s, four Kent State students were killed and eight injured by gun-toting National Guardsmen while the students were protesting the controversial Vietnam War.

The Watergate Scandal triggered shocking news in Washington that eventually brought down the Nixon White House.

A global energy crisis forced the American government to limit highway speeds to fifty-five miles an hour to reduce fuel consumption.

A nuclear-related accident at Three-Mile Island in Pennsylvania caused the evacuation of 100,000 people.

And by the end of the decade, the Soviet Union had invaded Afghanistan. That led to the boycott of the 1980 Moscow Summer Olympics by the United States and fifty-seven other countries.

11

RUNNING TO THE PROS, 1980-1989

Navy's fortunes against Army certainly had improved under George Welsh, and the Middies came into the decade in the midst of an unbeaten streak that would reach six—the longest it has had against the Cadets. Welsh's well-balanced team routed Army 33-6 in 1980, the Middies' third straight win by at least twenty-four points in the series. That victory punctuated how strong the Middies had become, with three straight winning records and two bowl appearances.

What was Welsh's secret?

He determined that his players needed more downtime during the week to help them juggle schedules that included heavy doses of classwork, studying, and football practices. So Welsh readjusted the time frames for meetings and what he called "mental preparation." He also scaled back the physicality of practice sessions.

A superb recruiter, Welsh's work in the late 1970s paid off with a solid core of veterans. Eddie Meyers, one of the great runners in academy history, was the star. Meyers was nearly as unstoppable in the 1980 romp as he was the previous year. The son of a retired Army officer was so impressive that pro scouts became interested. Meyers would serve his five-year military hitch, but each summer from 1982–1987 he would take his leave from the Marines and attend the Atlanta Falcons' training camp.

"Before college, I didn't think I had the talent, but I developed in college and got better," he said. "Then pro scouts thought I had the potential to play in the NFL. Once they said that, I gained more confidence in myself."

Meyers had hoped the Marine Corps would transfer him from San Diego to near Atlanta so he could more easily pursue a pro career. Or even have his military stint deferred while he tried to make the NFL, something that Navy star running back Napoleon McCallum would achieve later in the decade.

He was bitter about the double standard.

"It's hard to understand how two services cannot have the same policy," Meyers told the Associated Press in 1986. "Apparently, the Navy follows the order of the Secretary of the Navy but the Marines are more interested in the tough-guy image they want to uphold.

"There are other ways I could serve out my commitment and serve my country. I should be given what's due me at this point. It's fair and reasonable that I be given the same treatment Napoleon has received. I really feel I'm getting a raw deal and I just want things to be fair."

Meyers never made it in the NFL.

Neither did Gerald Walker, who scored the only Army touchdown in the 1980 game against Navy. Four years earlier, Walker was serving in South Korea after enlisting in the Army. His journey from soldier in Southeast Asia to West Point running back was a curious one because Walker didn't even play football in high school in South Carolina. And he never had any designs on attending the academy until some of his officers in Korea suggested he try.

Walker would finish his career two years later as one of Army's career rushing leaders, ahead of even Doc Blanchard. He was a 1,000-yard rusher in 1981, with eight touchdowns.

He also was one of Army's first great black players.

Walker barely played a role in the 1981 contest, injuring his leg early in the game. That match was noteworthy for several reasons. It was the only game in a six-year span that Navy did not beat Army. It was the final game coached by Welsh before he left for Virginia. And, unless NCAA rules are changed, it was the last time Army and Navy would tie.

The game ended 3-3, but it seemed almost like an Army victory considering how the Cadets recently had been dominated in the series.

In a sloppy offensive game, both teams excelled on defense, with tenacious pursuit and powerful tackles that jarred ball carriers and pass catchers all afternoon.

"Typical Army-Navy," Welsh said. "They began hitting hard on the first play and did so until the final play."

It was the first game without either team scoring a touchdown since 1934.

That changed quickly in 1982 and again in 1983. The Middies registered two more routs—winning in 1983 at the Rose Bowl as the game headed to the West Coast for the first time. It didn't seem to matter that Welsh was gone. One reason for Navy's potency was McCallum, who would set twenty-six school records in his sensational career. If he wasn't Bellino or Staubach—no Heismans on his résumé—McCallum still was one of the best backs in academy history, even in the history of both academies.

"Napoleon McCallum is as difficult to defend as any back in

the nation," Army coach Jim Young said after the 1985 game, a 17-7 Navy win. "His power and his determination are what you expect from a great athlete, and he is a great athlete."

McCallum's 217-yard rushing performance in 1985 showed his value after he missed the previous Army-Navy game and the Cadets won 28-11.

"The big thing they did was control the ball," said Army linebacker Larry Biggins. "We're supposed to be big on ball control, but we couldn't stop him from getting his 4–5 yards. Every play, 4–5 yards."

When Army had broken its slide in 1984, Navy was without McCallum, who had broken his leg early in the season. Indeed, McCallum was granted a redshirt year, allowing him to suit up in 1985, when he rushed for 1,327 yards and scored fifteen touchdowns.

Never—never—had the Naval Academy allowed a player to compete beyond his graduation date, a practice routine at nearly all Division I-A schools. "We had an obligation to support him after all the support he has provided for the Naval Academy and the Navy itself in recent years," said Rear Adm. Charles Larson, the academy superintendent. "He has been one of the most heralded athletes at the academy in the past two decades and has accrued for this institution an immeasurable amount of favorable recognition."

He kept doing that in his professional career. A 1986 fourth-round draft pick, McCallum made the Raiders and had 536 yards rushing while commuting from his ensign duties in Long Beach, California, to team practices back in the days when the Raiders were in Los Angeles. "Considering his schedule, he's been remarkable," Raiders coach Tom Flores said. "You have to be a unique person to handle the schedule he has. He certainly has handled it well at a time when we needed a running back with Marcus Allen's injury. He really stepped in and performed quite well."

Unfortunately for McCallum and the Raiders, he would spend the rest of the decade out of the NFL. New Secretary of the Navy James H. Webb, whose tenure lasted less than a year, revoked all special accommodations for military personnel to play professional sports.

McCallum, like Meyers before him, was crushed. "I don't like to have to defend myself," McCallum said of Webb's decision. "I feel everything I've done was in vain. It wasn't appreciated. I put a lot of effort and time in ensuring that what I did last year would work. From all indications, it did work. Everybody is happy except the new secretary." He finally rejoined the Raiders in 1990 after completing his military commitment. But he never was the same player and McCallum's pro career ended in the 1994 opener when he severely injured his right leg.

After McCallum, yet another superb running back grabbed the spotlight in the Army-Navy rivalry: West Point's Mike Mayweather. As a freshman in 1987, when Army won its second of three straight in the series, Mayweather rushed for 119 yards—a harbinger of his role in the rivalry. "I wasn't exactly calm before that game," Mayweather said. "It was more like my head was spinning, I was so high, sky high. The coaches had to tell me to relax at halftime."

Mayweather was the hub of a ground attack that gained 315 yards on seventy-two carries. Army threw only four times, but wore down the Middies.

It was more of the same the next year, although Mayweather was contained, gaining forty-one yards. But the Cadets finished off a 9-2 season by earning a Sun Bowl bid and winning the Commander in Chief's Trophy. There were only twenty total

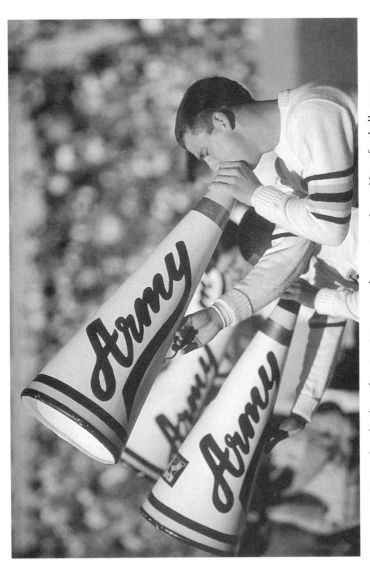

Army cheerleaders shouting into megaphones at an Army-Navy football game.
Bob Krist/CORBIS

West Point students celebrate victory over the Navy team in 1986.
Bob Krist/CORBIS

passes in the Cadets' 20-15 victory; Army ran sixty-five times for 246 yards.

By his junior season, Mayweather was a marked man for opponents. Stop him and you could beat the Cadets. The problem: few could stop Mayweather, who would become Army's career rushing leader—better even than Mr. Inside and Mr. Outside—during the 1989 season. Mayweather ran for 1,176 yards, setting an Army record. He gained eighty-four yards against Navy, but could not carry the Corps to victory in the first Army-Navy matchup at the New Jersey Meadowlands. Instead, it was Navy quarterback Alton Grizzard who played the hero's role.

Commander in Chief's Trophy.
Courtesy of the United States Military Academy

His three fourth-down conversions keyed the Middies' 19-17 win that was secured on Frank Schenk's 32-yard field goal with eleven seconds remaining.

Mayweather would get another victory in his final year at the Point, a 30-20 victory in 1990 in which he ran for eighty-seven yards, but often was a decoy as Willie McMillian surged for a career-high 195 yards.

He concluded his career with 4,299 yards. "I never expected it to turn out like this," Mayweather said. "I thought I'd probably play special teams or reserves until my junior year or so."

He wasn't looking back when his stint along the Hudson ended. Indeed, there was much more to think about with the clouds of war gathering in the Middle East. "You don't want to think about there being a war or getting shot at. Nobody does. But the reality of it is that war is what we've been trained for," Mayweather said. "If there is one thing you learn in four years at West Point, it is duty. And when duty calls, you have to go. In the final analysis, you're trained to be a manager of war."

12

REKINDLING THE RIVALRY, 1990-1999

By the early 1990s, the Army-Navy game wasn't quite so special to America. The rivalry lost some luster as both teams struggled to compile wins and Air Force gained success with an exciting option attack and some keynote victories.

While the Persian Gulf War in 1991 revitalized patriotism in the United States, that feeling didn't translate to the football games between Army and Navy. The national media seemed to lose interest in a matchup of also-rans, particularly with so many powerhouse teams in major conferences vying for attention. Why concentrate on two mediocre programs, even if they were Army and Navy, when you can sing the praises of Nebraska and Florida State, Miami and Tennessee?

But the media and the fans were being fooled. As recruiting scandals and criminal cases involving "student-athletes" cropped up from Coral Gables to Seattle, America found it needed a respite. It needed integrity and truth and commitment on fall Saturday afternoons.

It needed Army-Navy, and the academies were there with the tonic. The sporting public rediscovered its greatest rivalry, thanks to a streak of momentous games that epitomized what a hallmark matchup Army-Navy is.

From 1992–1996, the Cadets and Midshipmen played classics decided by no more than four points. Army won them all, but more significant than the West Point winning streak was the rebirth of the series, which was tied 43-43-7 heading into 1992. "Those are maybe the five greatest games, even though Army won them all, in the history of Army-Navy football. As a package of games, they really captured the imagination," said Tony Roberts, who did radio play-by-play of each thriller to an enthralled nationwide audience. "They just grabbed the attention of the nation again. The public had respect for the game, but not the way it had been, and the media had a passing respect for the game.

"The game was traditional: Army-Navy is always there, played the same time of the year. But it wasn't in the spotlight as much. Then you get close games right down to the wire, winner take all, for the bragging rights, and everyone starts thinking about Army-Navy. The media caught on again, and the fans and the TV networks recognized it became a great game once again."

Four of Army's five consecutive victories came at the Vet in Philadelphia, with the other at Giants Stadium in New Jersey. Each was marked by player heroics or flops and controversial coaching decisions. And by the time Army won 28-24 in 1996, the rivalry was front-page news again.

Coming off a loss to an 0-10 Navy team in 1991—the Cadets were only 4-7 themselves—Army's resolve seemed unquestionable heading into the 1992 matchup. "It doesn't matter about the records," Army defensive back Mike McElrath said, "because when you play Navy you can always throw everything out the window. Last year proved that because they were 0-10 coming into the game and they pulled their game up."

The only problem was Army didn't pull up its game at the outset of the 1992 meeting, either. Resolve doesn't mean much when your strength becomes a weakness and the Cadets, one of the top rushing teams in the nation at 276 yards per game, gained just six yards overall in the first quarter and 174 rushing in the game. They fell behind 24-7 in the third quarter.

Another devastating loss to a weak Middies squad—they were 1-9 entering the game—appeared certain.

Except no one ever gives up in an Army-Navy game, and the Cadets' comeback would begin the rekindling of the series. When Gaylord Greene hauled in a 68-yard touchdown reception from Rick Roper—at that point the longest in the game's illustrious history—it lifted Army to within four points. Green's brother, Gil, watched from the other side; they were the first brothers on opposite teams in an Army-Navy game since Art Born (Navy) and Chuck Born (Army) in 1926.

Army faked the placement kick and holder Chris Shaw scored a two-point conversion, making it 24-22. Kicking specialist Pat Malcom later had his punt downed at the Navy 1 and the Middies couldn't move. Army took over at the Navy 32 with 2:15 to play, ready to steal away its biggest win of the season.

But three plays later, the Cadets weren't much closer and Malcom set up for a 44-yard field goal, which he sent rocketing through the uprights amid pandemonium on the Army sideline.

Until the Cadets spotted the yellow flag for delay of game.

"He grabbed me by the face mask and said, 'You've got to do it again,'" Malcom said of Shaw, his roommate with whom he'd had a fistfight earlier in the week during a touch football game. "I didn't know what he meant, and then I saw the flag."

A 49-yard kick was something entirely different for Malcom—the longest attempt of his career. And all that was on the line was the outcome of the Army-Navy game.

Malcom simply shrugged and booted another perfect kick. "The second kick was almost easier than the first because I had the feeling that I'd already done it before," Malcom said.

Army 25, Navy 24.

"I think this year's victory was won in last year's locker room," said Army coach Bob Sutton, whose first Army-Navy game was the 1991 flop. "We did not want to go back through this again."

Instead, it was Navy suffering. And it would get worse the next year.

This time, the Cadets owned the lead and the Middies would rely on a kicker to snatch away the glory. Only the Navy kicker was not a seasoned veteran like Malcom, but a virtually untested freshman, Ryan Bucchianieri.

Just a month after earning the job, Bucchianieri was called on to beat Army with a chip shot, an 18-yard field goal in the final seconds. Navy set him up for such heroics by rallying from a 16-0 deficit.

The Middies had taken the Giants Stadium field on a dank day in a funk after learning of the murder of one of Navy's best all-time players, Alton Grizzard, days earlier. Coach George Chaump broke down when he told the team. "It was a nightmare," said Navy quarterback Jim Kubiak.

At the beginning of the contest, Army asserted its ground attack, appropriately enough. Roper's nine-yard run in the third quarter made it 16-0.

Then Navy, perhaps inspired by the memory of Grizzard, responded behind Kubiak, its junior leader. Kubiak found

Damon Dixon on passes of thirty-six, nineteen, and sixteen yards, then after scoring on a fourth-down rollout from the 3, he hit Dixon for the two-point conversion. The Brigade was rocking, and when Army fumbled the kickoff, Kubiak passed eight yards to Jim Mill to make it 16-14. But the two-point try failed when receiver Michael Jefferson dropped a handoff on a reverse. "He could have walked into the end zone backward," Roberts said.

Army was tiring and the nation's top rushing team couldn't move the ball in the wet conditions. Wet conditions were perfect for the Middies, of course.

Billy James ran six times for sixty yards and Navy relentlessly reached the Army 3, where Chaump made a huge blunder. Rather than continue their aggressive play and go for a touchdown against the exhausted Cadets, the Middies turned it off. Two runs into the line and a spike preceded Bucchianieri's kick from a difficult angle. "I don't think any of us thought he'd miss from there," Roper admitted. "You hope and you know all kinds of crazy things can happen in this game. But you don't expect it."

Still, an eighteen-year-old with no experience in such situations needed a better approach from the coaching staff. It was a poor enough decision not to keep attacking, but Navy didn't even try to position the ball in the middle of the field.

Bucchianieri botched the attempt wide right, then stood upright and stared into the gloomy dusk as the Corps celebrated a wild win.

"I knew it would come down to that," he said. "It was a kick I have kicked a thousand times over my life and it just didn't come out the way I would have liked it."

Army kicker Rocco Wicks approached Bucchianieri after the game and "told him to hold his head high and not let it bother him. Who knows, in a couple of years, he might make the kick and win it for them. I hope he sticks with it."

The loss would stick with Navy for another twelve months, when it would again get an opportunity to end its season more positively. And, again, everything would fall apart in another tight loss.

Both Army, ravaged by injuries, and Navy were 3-7 heading into their big game, but after two intense and thrilling performances in the previous years, the rivalry began receiving proper attention. Why, radio and television and this newfangled thing called the Internet were promoting Army-Navy as something worth watching.

Which, of course, the 1994 game was—in much the same way as its two scintillating predecessors. The star of this one was, yes, a kicker: Army's Kurt Heiss, who wasn't even a regular until midseason. But before he could nail a 52-yarder, the longest of his career by fifteen yards, Heiss had to wait for Army to make a comeback.

Navy led 14-10 at halftime behind the throws of Kubiak, the Middies' career passing leader. He set the tempo on the very first play when he hit Jefferson for thirty-two yards. Army quarterback Ronnie McAda had a brilliant 37-yard scamper on which he initially dropped the ball deep in the backfield. McAda later broke a 44-yard run, setting up Army's go-ahead touchdown for a 19-14 lead. The Middies responded with one of the series' most exciting plays, with tight end Kevin Hickman taking a screen pass and eluding tacklers down the sideline for a 56-yard score. When the two-point conversion failed not once but, after an Army penalty, twice, it was 20-19 for Navy.

Sticking with the run—the Cadets would gain 373 yards on sixty-eight carries—Army pushed toward the end zone. Kevin Vaughn rushed for eighty yards in the second half alone. "I didn't feel like they could stop the run," McAda said. "By the fourth quarter, they were worn out. That made it easy."

But not quite easy enough. The Cadets could get no closer

than the Navy 35 with just over six minutes to go. Out trotted Heiss, who regularly kicked longer field goals in practice, even if he couldn't see if they were good. Heiss' eyesight was so poor—"20-5,000 in the right, 20-800 in the left," he acknowledged—he had no idea if long-range field goals were true.

This one was true.

"When did I know I made it?" he said after a 22-20 win. "When my teammates mobbed me."

Navy couldn't mount a charge following Heiss' hefty boot, and Army had a three-game winning streak by a total of five points.

"It's the greatest feeling in the world," Sutton said. "There is no better feeling than going into the locker room after beating Navy."

The coach was getting used to it. He also was accustomed to winning in the final moments, and the 1995 game would be no exception. Why should it be? This is Army-Navy.

The Cadets' string against the Middies would reach four, the longest in 48 years, thanks to some more odd coaching. This time it was Charlie Weatherbie, who replaced Chaump in 1995.

Navy also missed out on its first winning season since 1982, winding up 5-6 after Weatherbie got adventurous, then his defense disintegrated.

The Middies did have another freshman kicker, Tom Venderhorst, but he'd already made two field goals and his team led 13-7 with 8:23 remaining at Philadelphia. Behind their elusive, innovative quarterback, Chris McCoy, the Midshipmen reached the Army 1 on fourth down. Simple call, right? Kick the field goal, take a nine-point lead and force the Cadets, who had displayed little offensive flair, to get a touchdown and a field goal.

Instead, Weatherbie opted to go for it. The Navy way? Perhaps in other circumstances, but here?

"That's a good question," Weatherbie said. "I'm sure I'll be kicking myself in the tail until next year about it. . . . That was a very, very poor tactical error on my part. Hindsight's 20-20 though. If I had to do it over, I'd kick it."

McCoy's pass into the end zone fell incomplete and the entire Brigade on hand seemed to sense what would come next. "There were a lot of things going through my mind," Weatherbie explained. "We had the ball on the left hash marks, which is a tough angle. I thought we would have a receiver open—and we did. If we get the score, the game's over. If we don't, they still have ninety-nine yards to go."

And ninety-nine yards they went, gaining momentum with each succeeding play—and each cheer, louder and louder, from the Corps. McAda, though, was sacked for a 12-yard loss on a third-down play, pushing the ball back to the Navy 29 in the final two minutes. Faced with fourth-and-24, McAda, better known for his running, came up with one of the great clutch plays in Army-Navy history when he threw a perfect 28-yard pass to John Graves. Two plays later, John Conroy bulled into the end zone and the extra point made it 14-13.

"We just knew we were going to come back. You must have that attitude. We did," said Conroy.

It's the never-give-up attitude that has served the Corps and the Brigade so well after these athletes leave the academy. The lessons learned—on the field and watching from the stands as their classmates perform so bravely—never are lost.

The sequence of losses, though, weighed heavily on this group of Middies, particularly the seniors. "The first thing anybody asks you when they hear you went to Navy is, 'Did you beat Army?'" defensive end Andy Person said. "For me to be able to say that is so important."

But it was not to be.

"As a freshman, you never imagine that you'll get swept," said safety Joe Speed, who had ten tackles. "Now that it's happened, I really just don't know what to say. What can you say? We failed. We didn't beat Army. That is something I'll have to live with."

As would the rest of the Middies for another year. And the exhilarating nature of the games had assured that America's greatest rivalry would remain front and center on the crowded sports calendar. In fact, it had become such a spotlight game that President Clinton attended in 1996, the first time the chief executive showed up since Gerald Ford in 1974. "Both the Secretary of the Navy and the Secretary of the Army have tried every year to get me to come, and something has prevented it every time," Clinton said. "I had the day open. I wanted to be here, and I'm very proud to be here." Wearing a purple button saying "Army vs. Navy—Joint Winners,"—purple is the neutral color for the armed services and America's No. 1 fan can't show any preference when Army meets Navy—Clinton sat with the Brigade for the first half and with the Corps for the second.

He was treated to yet another classic, something that was becoming routine for Army-Navy. Adding to the excitement and intrigue was both teams heading into the contest with winning records. Army was 9-1 and Navy 8-2, and an Independence Bowl bid was on the line. Clinton was inspired by the likes of Navy linebacker Clint Bruce, whose father Richard died when he was in high school, never seeing his son complete the journey through Annapolis. "For me it was real easy," Bruce said. "I want to be a SEAL. I thought the academy would be the best place for me to pursue that. I wanted to take care of my mom and sister. That was important to me. When I graduate here, I'll already have a good job.

"That's not to say it's not hard when a 120-pound guy is

yelling at you," Bruce added of academy life. "But it helps prepare you for what the world is going to be like. And I look at it as I'm sacrificing the years eighteen to twenty-two, while most people are sacrificing twenty-two to twenty-six getting their careers established. I'm going to have a job, an exciting job, waiting for me."

He wanted to head to that job with a victory over Army, something Bruce never had tasted. And his prospects were promising when the Middies moved ahead 21-3 in the second period. Then McAda, the engineer of the length-of-the-field drive to victory the previous year, broke Navy's hearts again. His 44-yard touchdown run started the Army rally to the biggest comeback victory in series history. Bobby Williams broke free for an 81-yard run, the second-longest in the ninety-seven years the game had been played. Demetrius Perry's 3-yard run provided the winning points, and Garland Gay's interception clinched yet another West Point celebration as Army held on for a 28-24 victory.

"I'm going out with my family and my friends and my teammates and I'm going to hit the town, because I haven't done it yet after an Army-Navy game," McAda said after rushing for 134 yards and passing for 116, lifting him past some very select company in Army football annals: McAda finished his Army career with 533 total yards in three games against Navy, beating Glenn Davis' 359 yards.

"Watch out Philadelphia."

The Middies just wanted to get out of Philly, smarting from their longest slide in the series since the 1940s. Only one thing could boost their morale, and they'd have to wait another twelve months to seek it.

And get it.

Navy finally broke Army's streak with a 39-7 rout in 1997

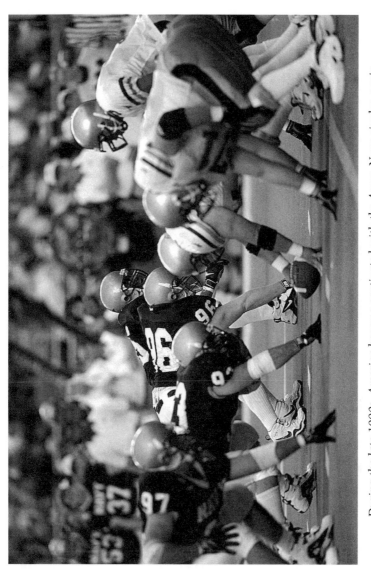

During the late 1990s, America became captivated with the Army-Navy rivalry again.

Duomo/CORBIS

Excited fans during the 1998 Army-Navy game.

Duomo/CORBIS

as quarterback McCoy rushed for 205 yards and accounted for four touchdowns.

Meanwhile, America once again had been captivated by Army-Navy football.

"To see the Cadets and the Midshipmen performing to the very limits of their ability for each other and their teams is a very rewarding and comforting feeling," Clinton said. "America's future is in very secure hands."

FALLEN MIDSHIPMEN

Two players had a major impact on the 1993 Army-Navy game: Alton Grizzard and Ryan Bucchianeri.

Grizzard was one of Navy's most accomplished players, a four-year starter and captain of the 1990 team. He went on to train with the Navy SEALS and, before a 1992 game with Tulane, the former quarterback spoke to the Middies, who were 0-7 at the time. The inspired players rolled over the Green Wave for Navy's only victory that season.

Grizzard was just 1-3 against Army, but he'd become something of a legend among the Brigade—and not just for his football accomplishments, although he was the school's career total offense leader with 5,666 yards rushing and passing when he graduated. The fourth player in Navy history to rush for 2,000 yards, as a senior, Grizzard set a record with twelve touchdown passes.

"If there's ever a Midshipman who left here and was going to become an admiral, it was Alton Grizzard," said Navy's athletic director at the time, Jack Lengyel. "He was a true leader. When he went into the huddle, he commanded respect—and he got it."

Three days before the Army game in 1993, Grizzard and another officer, Kerryn O'Neill, were shot to death inside the bachelor officers quarters at a southern California

Naval base by George Smith, another Naval Academy graduate and O'Neill's ex-fiancé. Coach George Chaump, whose team had just lost four straight, delivered the tragic news to the Midshipmen, many of whom cried.

"Alton Grizzard was a motivational person," fullback Brad Stramanak said. "I don't think he would want us to dwell on this. He would want us to go out and beat Army."

As if they needed any more incentive, the Middies wore "GRIZ" on their gold helmets for the contest.

But the Middies instead were pushed around by the Cadets for much of the game at Giants Stadium. Army built a 16-0 lead on a damp day and appeared in control—just as Navy did the previous year, when the Cadets stormed back from a 24-7 hole to win on Patmon Malcom's 49-yard field goal with twelve seconds remaining.

Then again, this was Army-Navy.

The Middies scored two touchdowns in two minutes early in the fourth quarter. With four-and-a-half minutes remaining, they took the ball at their 21-yard line and began marching toward the Army end zone. And victory.

At the Army 3, Chaump got conservative. Although quarterback Jim Kubiak petitioned the coach to aggressively go for a touchdown, fearing the wet conditions would make a field goal problematic, Chaump ordered two runs and a spike that left the ball at the 1. Then he turned to freshman kicker Ryan Bucchianeri.

A month earlier, "Boocch" had become the regular kicker. A high school all-American in Pennsylvania, he'd made two field goals against Notre Dame in his first game. He understood the pressure of the situation.

"I felt confident," he said. "I believed I would make the kick."

So did the Middies in the crowd, who already were leaving their seats, ready to celebrate on the field.

From a difficult angle—Chaump later was criticized for not running the ball into the middle of the field on third down to make the field goal try easier—Bucchianeri missed wide right. From eighteen yards.

Army held on 16-14.

"I did the best I could, that's how I feel," Bucchianeri said. "I need to put it out of my mind, but I will go to sleep tonight knowing I did my best. It didn't turn out the way I would have liked, though."

Nor would the rest of his career.

Although he received dozens of letters and notes of encouragement from Midshipmen, officers, even admirals, Bucchianeri's football career spiraled precipitously. So did much of his life at the academy.

Bucchianeri kicked again the next year, missing—wide right—on a 37-yard field goal early in a 22-20 loss. Making matters worse for him, Army's Kurt Heiss, whose poor eyesight made the goalposts a blur from such a distance, nailed a career-long 52-yarder for the decisive points.

"A 50-yarder to win the Army-Navy game is a dream come true," Bucchianeri told the media. "But it wasn't me kicking it. I had to watch somebody else kicking it."

He would do lots of watching for the rest of his stay at Annapolis. Even though a new coaching staff took over in 1995, Bucchianeri would never attempt another field goal in a game. A bit of an outcast, he became the object of derision from classmates throughout his final two years at the academy. Someone even coined the term "Boocched" for an attempt (at anything) gone awry, and it caught on among the Middies.

For much of those last two years in the Brigade, Bucchianeri didn't suit up for games. Today, when his name comes up in Army-Navy conversation, it nearly always is accompanied by "wide right."

13

NOW MORE THAN EVER, 2000-2004

In the twenty-first century, America needed Army-Navy more than ever. Naturally, the Corps and the Brigade delivered. They delivered as students, as militarymen, as athletes, as Americans. With the United States facing the deepest threats in decades to its peace and security, the brave young men and women at West Point and Annapolis embraced their missions.

While it's absurd to believe football was a pivotal component of those missions, it is just as ridiculous to dismiss the importance to academy life of the Army-Navy series. Particularly in the new millennium.

"This game is an ideal," said Todd Berry, Army's coach from 2000–2003. "Motivation is not an issue. . . . This program, this place, is aspiring to do great things. All the time, in every place."

In Annapolis, too. "We'll be enemies on the field," Navy

quarterback Aaron Polanco said in 2002. "But when all is said and done, we're one. We are a brotherhood."

Never has that been more true and more critical than in the last few years.

Navy carried a two-game success string and had won three of four meetings with Army heading into the 2001 game, less than three months after the September 11 terrorist attacks and weeks after American troops began fighting in Afghanistan. The contest already held some significance as the final Army-Navy game in the Vet. But it grew in notability as Americans searched for a rallying point.

"I don't know how the game could be more important to us, but it is more important (to the public)," said Rick Lantz, who coached Navy against Army in 2001. "People look a little differently now at the military, police, and firefighters. I think there will be great pride in the stands."

Added Navy captain Jake Bowen: "Football is a great stress relief. While there are things going on of greater global significance, sports is still important. It's a way to unite people."

Including the president—George W. Bush attended the game, as much to send a message that life in the United States was going on as normally as possible. "I have no fear coming to the game," he told the nation. "What I'm really here to do is to say to the country how proud I am of our military folks.

"My mind is on the game today, but my mind is elsewhere, too. My mind is with the men and women who wear our uniform as we wage a noble cause. Know that our cause is just because it is right. Make no mistake about it—we will prevail."

Prevail because of the men who took the field that Saturday, and every Saturday for more than a hundred years. Men who believed unflinchingly in that cause. Men who always gave their all for that cause, many times making the ultimate sacrifice.

"I think because of what happened, people will look at this game and say, 'Hey, these guys will be going over there next year, doing what we're seeing on television,' and they respect that, which is good," Army linebacker Brian Zickefoose said.

"You know the drill, you know the deal," Polanco added. "We're blessed to play football now. But you know what you signed up for."

More than usual, the players recognized how much the game meant to their peers, former Cadets and Middies now stationed overseas, hoping for a little respite, a little relief from home. A little football.

Navy hadn't played much good football during the 2001 season, going 0-9 heading into the Army contest. A defeat would give the Midshipmen their first all-losing season since going 0-1 in 1883. In 2000, they avoided a winless record with a 30-28 victory over Army.

Army was 2-8 coming into the 2001 game. Its decision to join Conference USA in 1998 was beginning to wreak havoc on the program, as was Berry's infatuation with a wide-open offense. Army simply couldn't attract the kind of athletes to run such an attack, nor could it compete with conference schools that didn't place nearly the emphasis on education as the academy did.

None of that mattered, of course, with the Brigade on the other side of the field.

The Cadets came up with big play after big play in a 26-17 victory. Although President Bush left in the third quarter, he was around long enough to see Omari Thompson's 96-yard return of the second-half kickoff and a freshman, Ardell Daniels, romp sixty yards for a touchdown. Indeed, Daniels' 131-yard rushing performance made him the first freshman to earn MVP honors.

"It was the greatest feeling in my life," said Daniels.

Feeling great was something every American could appreciate. Good vibes were rare that autumn.

"Obviously, the 11th of September changed all our lives," Berry said. "This game had more significance because of that." To everyone—players, coaches, soldiers, sailors, presidents.

"With everything that has been going on, people are reaching out to touch something with the Army and Navy," Army center Dustin Plumadore said. "I know people are really concerned about what's going on overseas. They're not getting an opportunity to reach out and touch those soldiers. Us playing this game was a way to reach out, to look in the crowd and see future and current soldiers."

And to be proud.

By the next time the academies faced off in 2002, Navy had a new coach, Paul Johnson, but not much more success. The Middies were 1-10 entering the meeting at the Meadowlands.

Army's gridiron spiral was in full force, too, and the Cadets also were 1-10. Could America find interest in such a matchup?

With a pending military action in Iraq, and with a growing admiration for "Our Troops," of course it could.

"We represent the purest form of college football," said Army assistant coach Joe Ross, a former player who fought in Kosovo. "We're taking twenty credits, we're playing Division I-A football, and we are preparing for a profession in the military. I took great pride in being an Army football player. It's one of the hardest things anyone can do. I went to Ranger school and it was a piece of cake because of how Army football had prepared me."

What fans never could have been prepared for was an unprecedented scoring splurge from the Middies, who whipped Army 58-12. Navy's points total was the most in the historic series. Quarterback Craig Candeto looked like Roger Staubach and Joe Bellino rolled into one unstoppable force as he ran for a school-record six touchdowns and threw for another. Navy's 508 yards on offense and 421 on the ground set game marks.

Only Navy's 51-0 victory in 1973 was more lopsided. "I feel like we let our families down and our teammates," said Cadets team captain Clarence Holmes. "We represent the Army and there is a lot of pain going on. At the same time, we have to keep our heads high and be strong for the Army, be leaders and see this through."

One day before the game, Johnson brought his team to Ground Zero in Manhattan "to see what they would be fighting for in the future."

Were they inspired by the trip, or were the Middies just that much stronger than the Cadets? Let Candeto explain.

"We're not just playing for the academy," Candeto said. "We're playing for all the people who have fought and died for our freedoms. It's bigger than us. We're playing on a field for people who are fighting overseas for us. Football is small in the whole realm of things. It makes you play that much harder. It's about service and duty."

By 2003, service and duty for many members of the armed forces meant a tour in the Iraq war zone. Chad Jenkins, who played quarterback for Army with a damaged knee in 2001, commanded a platoon there. The second lieutenant was in charge of night patrols that searched for explosives. He was one of four West Point classmates who played football and, after graduation, were dispatched to Iraq.

"They don't come any better than Chad Jenkins," said former Army offensive coordinator John Bond, recalling a player who had few great athletic attributes but more perseverance and dedication than almost anyone he'd met. "He squeezed every ounce of ability out of that 175-pound body every day, every week. He got more out of himself than anybody I've ever been around. He played hurt and he played healthy and all points in between, and you never would know the difference."

Jenkins recalled a particularly gruesome scene on November 2, 2003, in Iraq, telling the Associated Press about a downed helicopter that killed sixteen soldiers: "It was just a horrific day. We were eating breakfast when we got the call that the Chinook was down and that victims were receiving fire. We got over there in fifteen to twenty minutes and set up a perimeter. There was no small fire, so we sent in guys to provide first aid and get IDs. It was something you train for, but hope you never have to do.

"Then we had to stay an additional five days so that no looters came to take away pieces of the Chinook. Those five days, being around the crash site, were the worst."

Graham White, the Cadets punter in 1999 and considered a pro prospect, was deployed in Operation Iraqi Freedom, too. He was injured and saw two comrades killed by a car bomb explosion in Baghdad.

Aaron Rigby, who played linebacker for the Middies in three Army-Navy games in the 1990s, did two tours of the Middle East. He watched the 2000 and 2001 contests while at sea. "My first tour was the year before 9/11, and we were near Yemen in 2000 when the USS *Cole* was bombed," Rigby said. "You know an attack like that always is a possibility and you're trained for it at the academy and afterward. But you never think it will happen on your watch."

Rigby's ship, the USS *Anchorage*, arrived in Yemen two days after the bombing to perform aid and relief for the *Cole*'s crew members. He bumped into a former Middies teammate, Kyle Turner, although not much reminiscing went on then. He watched the 2000 game onboard the *Anchorage* off the coast of Kuwait. There was only one other Annapolis graduate on the ship.

"My commanding officer, Dave Angood, played football at Michigan and played in the Rose Bowl, so we were watching games throughout the year. To watch Army-Navy, it was good to have someone who could relate to the feelings of being a former player.

"It is really odd. You watch what would be a noon game that is on at midnight or 1 A.M. in the Middle East. Reception can be kind of sketchy; you might not be in position where the ship can get the game. Luckily, we were able to get it.

"I'll tell you it is a real morale booster to watch it on a ship with everyone else—the troops can rally around each other."

In a world increasingly filled with fear and turmoil, with the scope of terrorism now an everyday threat to Americans, a willingness—indeed, a need—to embrace patriotism, to pay tribute to the people who defend our hard-won freedoms, is embodied by the Cadets and Midshipmen. Never is that more true than when Army meets Navy in football.

"This game is important anyway, but it gives it a little extra," Johnson said of the Iraq war. "Last night at dinner we had a flag sent to us that flew over the airport in Baghdad. That they thought enough to do that, it tells you the military overseas and everywhere can stop for three–four hours and it's like being home."

When they met in 2003, Navy's fortunes had turned under Johnson. At 7-4, the Middies already owned a Houston Bowl bid, and their option offense was sensational. These Midshipmen could stage a ground assault every general at West Point would envy, sparked by two 1,000-yard runners, a first for Navy.

Running back Kyle Eckel and quarterback Candeto had a spanking new stage on which to display their dominance against the Cadets, who were trying to avoid the first 0-13 season in college football history. The game was the first for Army

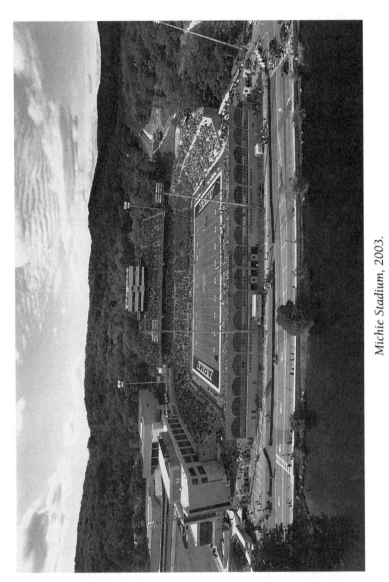

Michie Stadium, 2003.
Courtesy of the United States Military Academy

and Navy at Lincoln Financial Field, the new home of the Philadelphia Eagles.

It was a mismatch. Navy scored twenty-seven straight points, with Eckel's bursts of twelve and sixteen yards in the fourth quarter punctuating the 34-6 rout. Eckel rushed for 152 yards and Eric Roberts also had two touchdowns. Navy gained 359 yards on the ground.

Navy also earned the Commander in Chief's Trophy, awarded to the team with the best record in games among the three service academies, for the first time since 1981—six coaches ago.

"It's huge," Candeto said. "It's something none of us have experienced."

Halfway across the globe, members of the armed forces in Iraq watched the game, many on a tape delay, which didn't matter much—they were kind of busy when the game itself was played.

Soldiers at Champion Base in Ar Ramadi were treated to a tailgate party as they watched Navy's victory. The 82nd Airborne Division's band was flown in to play during the festivities and played both traditional holiday songs and popular music, a welcome break from the hostilities surrounding the American troops.

There were only a few complaints: that Army lost, and that drinking beer had been outlawed.

The loss, Army's fourth in five games against its biggest rival, left Cadets interim coach John Mumford with an 0-7 record. Berry had been fired after the first six defeats of 2003.

"There's a good team in there in those kids. I couldn't get it out of them," Mumford said. "They need confidence. They need to win. They are a great group of young men. It's been an honor to work with them."

14

WAR ZONE:

THE SEAL AND THE SOLDIER

A SEAL's Story

First he was a Navy football player. Then he was a Navy SEAL.

First he traveled by land, then by sea.

First he helped sink Army, then he helped sink terrorists.

Now Brian Drechsler applies lessons he learned from his college football days to his everyday life in the military.

"Football by far and large was the biggest developer for me as a leader," he said. "It teaches you about true teamwork—that there are other people counting on you, playing injured and taking the pain for that guy across from you in the huddle who is feeling the same thing."

Since playing football for Navy in the 1990s, Drechsler has embarked on a wide-ranging military career that has taken him to some of the world's hottest trouble spots. He has been deployed in Iraq since September 2004.

"Unfortunately, I can't get into specifics of our operations out here," he writes in an e-mail. "But I am very busy and having fun."

Drechsler remembered the last time he stepped on a football field for Navy. It was the 1997 season and the Middies routed the Cadets 39-7. It was thrilling, but also bittersweet for Drechsler.

"I was happy that we had won, but that feeling was almost overshadowed by the emptiness of knowing that was the last football game that I would ever play," he said.

Drechsler came out of a strong football program at Upper St. Clair High School in Pittsburgh.

"We were a very successful team, actually ranked No. 4 in the nation my senior year," he recalled. "I was the starting left tackle."

Why did he choose Navy?

"I had two cousins that went there. David Papak, USNA '76, started at defensive tackle for three years and recently was promoted to brigadier general in the Marine Corps. When I was ten years old, my dad took me to visit him in Annapolis. I fell in love with it and wanted to go there ever since."

At Navy, he lettered from 1995–1997. He played on Navy's first winning team since 1982, the 1996 squad that went 9-3 and beat California in the Aloha Bowl. The only problem with that season was the Middies lost to Army, same as they did in 1995.

"We lost two nail-biters," Drechsler remembers. "In '95, we were up 13-7, we had a fourth and goal with a few minutes left in the game. We decided to go for it (and failed). Then Army had that epic 99-yard drive to beat us (14-13).

"The following year, we lost again, 28-24, dropping two

passes in the end zone. We approached that '97 game different as a group. It was our senior year and we wanted to go out winners. We knew we could win, but the whole week of practice was: it doesn't have to be close, and it wasn't."

Navy 39, Army 7.

"It was a great way to end our careers."

Drechsler said the excitement of the Army-Navy game was unparalleled for him.

"It is pure madness," he said of the week leading up to the game.

As for the pressure, especially from Navy's upper echelon: "There are a lot of hierarchy that could care less if the football team goes 1-10, as long as that win is against Army," Drechsler said. "I remember being extremely nervous my sophomore year. It was a shock to me. I was getting e-mails from alumni I had never heard of."

Drechsler graduated from Annapolis in May 1998. In January 1999, he reported to Basic Underwater Demolition/SEAL School in Coronado, California. He graduated in August 1999 after "six months of hell."

Then, "As if I hadn't had enough of the Army, I went to their basic airborne school in Fort Benning, Georgia."

He then reported to SEAL Team FIVE, "where I was the third officer of DELTA Platoon."

"I was fortunate to join the ranks of a very close and personal friend and former teammate, Clint Bruce, USNA '97," he added. "Clint was the assistant officer in charge, and I couldn't be happier to be doing this job with such a great guy."

Drechsler was on deployment in Guam when he first got the news of the terrorist attacks in New York and Washington on September 11, 2001.

"I will never forget it," he said. "It was 1 A.M. there, and I was woken up by Clint Bruce. I was shocked, angry, and I wanted revenge. Three weeks later I was in Kuwait and patrolling the Persian Gulf."

Drechsler's job was to board noncompliant vessels "that were smuggling either Iraqi oil or al Qaeda that were trying to escape."

Drechsler later served in the Pacific before training at the Army's free-fall parachute school. By then, he had been elevated to officer-in-charge of SEAL Team FIVE ALFA Platoon. In September 2004, his unit was deployed to Iraq.

There, he has found a "huge bond between football players from USNA."

"It's hard to describe, but it is a brotherhood. Football is tough enough, but when you add to it the rigors of military life, it is even more difficult. When you go through that, it does change you and you have no choice but to become extremely proud and loyal to those who have gone through it with you."

The results of the Army-Navy game, of course, is one of the most important bits of news they can get from the States.

"I have followed it when I could," Drechsler said. "I was actually out on operations during several of them. Over the communications net I would have our operations center pass me the score. That should indicate how important the game is."

Just as important as the relationships Drechsler has formed in his football and service careers.

"We were a bunch of guys that loved our country and loved to play football," he said. "Sure, we may have been an inch too short, a step too slow or a couple of pounds too light to get looked at by bigger schools.

"But come Saturday, you had better come to play or you were going to get beat. We were a team of brothers in every sense of the word."

A Soldier's Story

Imagine this: It's a black night in Iraq. You're flying an Apache attack helicopter at 200 mph. Guns are blazing at you from the ground just 50 feet below.

Army captain Ben Kotwica didn't have to imagine it. To him, it was all too real. "It can make for some interesting and exciting nights," said the ex-Army football player, "especially out there with it being a two-way range. It can make for some very tense situations."

After spending thirteen harrowing months in Iraq as a helicopter pilot, Kotwica had recently returned to the United States. Once the captain of an Army bowl team in 1996, Kotwica was now a captain in the military—a captain on his way to becoming a civilian.

"I'm going to coach at the prep school at Fort Monmouth," he said. "I coached there once when I was a lieutenant, as a graduate assistant. I'm transitioning out of the military, and I'm going to help Coach Ross win some football games. Hopefully, we can turn this Army-Navy thing around, too."

Bobby Ross, of course, became the head football coach at Army in 2004. The United States Military Academy Preparatory School (USMAPS) at Fort Monmouth, New Jersey, is a steppingstone to West Point for combat veterans, as well as high school graduates who need academic help. Of course, football is a big part of the USMAPS program, featuring a "Little Army-Navy Game" between prep schools for West Point and Annapolis.

As for being able to "turn around" Army-Navy, the recent dominance of the Middies in the football series certainly irks every soldier. Navy's victory in 2004 made it three straight for the Middies and five of the previous six.

Losing to Navy was something entirely foreign to Kotwica when he played linebacker and strong safety at Army in the 1990s, and also coached at USMAPS.

"I was 4-0 against Navy when I was at West Point, and I beat them when I was in prep school, so I was 5-0," Kotwica pointed out. "When I interviewed with Coach Ross, he was mentioning about turning this thing around and starting to win some. I said, coach, I really can't sympathize with you because I really don't know what it's like to lose to them."

And he has no intention of finding out. Kotwica played high school football in Chicago and like most young players from that area, hoped to play in the Big Ten or at Notre Dame. "The reality was that people loved what they saw on film, but when they met me in person, that was when videotape met reality," he said. "I was only a 5-10, 190/195-pound linebacker, and a little too small. I just wasn't quite fast enough to play free safety or strong safety in the Big Ten or Notre Dame.

"But Army stayed with me. Bob Sutton was there. I really felt a bond with him and his coaching staff and the players. I felt it was the right fit."

As a sophomore in 1994, Kotwica got his chance to play. Army beat Navy 22-20 that season as Kurt Heiss kicked a career-long 52-yard field goal with 6:19 to play.

Then in 1995, Army won again, 14-13, with the help of that 99-yard drive in the final minutes. Navy had failed to score from the Army 1 a few minutes before the Cadets' winning drive.

"Navy made the decision to go for it on fourth-and-1," Kotwica recalled. "They wanted to put a touchdown in. Chris McCoy, instead of running the ball, dropped back to pass and threw an incompletion and then we turned it the other way."

At one point during their drive, the Cadets were in a fourth-and-24. But Ronnie McAda completed a 28-yard pass to John

Graves for the first down, and Army scored on a short touchdown run by John Conroy with 1:03 left.

"We never really lost confidence," Kotwica said. "Even when it was fourth-and-24, there was always that feeling that somehow things were going to turn out that way."

Same thing in 1996 when Army trailed Navy 21-3 in the first half. The Cadets scored two quick touchdowns in the final 5:14 of the second period and went on to a 28-24 victory.

The Cadets stopped Navy twice on drives deep in their territory in the final minutes, the last on an interception by Garland Gay with 10 seconds remaining. In rallying from an 18-point deficit, Army made the series' greatest comeback. "You talk about excitement, being on the defensive end of the ball. Navy ended up having about eight shots inside our 10-yard line in a rainstorm in Philly."

Army later lost to Auburn in the Independence Bowl, but the season had already been a success. With victories over Navy and Air Force, the Cadets clinched their first outright Commander in Chief's Trophy since 1988. They finished the year with a 10-2 record, the last winning season for Army through 2004.

Kotwica did some coaching at prep school following graduation in 1997, then joined Army Aviation and went to flight school. Not long after that came a tour in Bosnia. "That was kind of hot. I did that for eight, nine months," he said.

Then he served in Korea for just over a year before returning to his base in Fort Hood, Texas, and his outfit, the First Cavalry Division.

Next stop: Iraq.

"It's a very dynamic environment . . . up and down. When we arrived in Iraq, we replaced the First Armored Division and we thought it was going to be a peacekeeping, stability operation, but that wasn't the case.

"About two weeks into it, we lost a couple of pilots and we lost a helicopter that got shot down, and realized that peace-keeping stability turned into combat operations. We were pretty much involved in that for the length of my deployment there. There were events in different cities, not only Baghdad, but Najaf down to the south, and Fallujah out to the West, that we all had a part of."

When fighting a war, there is "a lot of down time followed by very high spikes," Kotwica said. "It's kind of like a ferris wheel ride that's interrupted by the roller coaster every once in a while. When the roller coaster hits, you have to really be ready for it. We were at a base where we received mortar attacks, rocket attacks and that was probably the biggest thing. You just really never knew.

"Complacency was one thing that you just couldn't allow in your guys, and that was something that you had to fight against."

Even in times of war, and no matter where he has been in the world, Kotwica hasn't missed watching an Army-Navy game. In 2003, it was in Korea. When he arrived in Iraq, satellites were just becoming available for communications. During the 2004 Army-Navy game, fifteen or twenty guys crammed into a small room with sodas and a couple of pizzas and watched the action.

If only for a few hours, it relieved the stress of war and revived old memories of Kotwica's days at West Point.

Kotwica said his football experiences at Army were applicable to his experiences in Iraq. "There's a lot of carry-over between the things that happen on the athletic field and war. You learn things between the white lines, not only about yourself but about the guys next to you. The challenges you faced week in and week out make you better as an individual and better as a unit.

"Playing football isn't unlike going into battle. And when you're playing ballgames and you're shoulder to shoulder on Saturday against another team, that's kind of what it's like when we're flying out there and supporting the ground units. You're in that together."

Thanks to his role as a captain on the Army football team, Kotwica brought leadership qualities to the field of battle. "You held guys together in times that were tough, times when you kind of buckled the chinstrap or strapped on the helicopter. You got the job done," he said. "The ability to overcome challenges and overcome adversity and have a positive attitude is a carry-over of things I learned on the football field."

15

ARMY-NAVY LORE

Gone, and Still Forgotten

There were "Mr. Inside and Mr. Outside," the "Lonely End" . . . and then the "Forgotten Grenadiers."

The "Forgotten Grenadiers"? Maybe not as famous as the other great Army teams, but coach Earl Blaik thought they deserved a special place in legendary West Point football history, too.

"They would have given the Lonely Enders a tough time," Blaik once said, "and might even have operated respectably against B. and D."

"B. and D.," of course, were Doc Blanchard and Glenn Davis, the Heisman Trophy winners of the mid-1940s at Army. The "Lonely Enders" referred to the team in the late 1950s featuring Bill Carpenter, who was nicknamed the "Lonely End" when he lined up fifteen yards wide of the rest of the team. The unique new formation immediately captured the imagination of the football world.

As for the "Grenadiers," Blaik thought they featured "beautiful expositions of two-platoon football."

"Quarterbacked by Arnold Galiffa, they were undefeated and untied (9-0)," Blaik said in a 1959 interview in *Look* magazine. "They were superior as a unit, with great speed, power and spirit and considerable skill."

Proof of the "Grenadiers" greatness came in the 1949 game with Navy, a 38-0 Army victory. Not even the B. and D. and Lonely Enders teams could pull off such a rout in the rivalry.

Keeping a Promise

In the early part of the 1950s, Army was getting into a habit of losing to Navy. After dropping four of the previous five games to their arch rival, the Cadets hoped to break the habit in 1955.

It was the night before the game, and the Army team was staying at its usual place at the Manufacturers Country Club outside of Philadelphia. As was customary, Blaik took his team for the pre-taps stroll around the country club's golf course.

"I have grown weary of walking across the field to offer congratulations this year to Bennie Oosterbaan of Michigan, Ben Schartzwalder of Syracuse, and Jordan Olivar of Yale," Blaik told his underachieving players.

"Now, I'm not as young as I used to be and that walk tomorrow, before 100,000 people and 50 million on TV, to congratulate (Navy coach) Eddie Erdelatz, would be the longest I've ever taken."

The Cadets were silent until quarterback Don Holleder spoke up.

"Colonel, you are not going to take that walk tomorrow," he said.

Holleder was as good as his word as Army beat Navy 14-6 the next day.

And Blaik didn't have to cross the field. He merely walked off with a victory.

Hey, Who's Side Are You On, Anyway?

Here's a novelty: In 1942, Bob Woods played for Army in a 14-0 loss to Navy.

What's so unusual about that?

One year earlier, he had played 58 minutes to help Navy beat Army, 14-6.

"He thus becomes the first to win an Army star for appearing against Navy one year after winning a Navy star against Army," wrote Bob Considine in the November 29, 1942, issue of the *Washington Post*.

Woods made the switch of schools after apparent academic problems at Navy, and became a better student at Army.

Something else happened in the 1942 game that was also an anomaly:

Because of the war, the Army-Navy game was played at Thompson Stadium at Annapolis that year. Travel restrictions limited the crowd to 12,000, all of whom came within a twelve-mile radius.

The only representatives from West Point were the football team and three cheerleaders.

So Navy designated two of its brigades to cheer for Army.

The Army cheerleaders, aided by two cheerleaders from Navy, helped to pump up their enthusiasm.

Talk about Busy

In 1913, an excited record crowd of 40,000 attended the Army-Navy game at the Polo Grounds in New York. Among them was one particular fan who had made a long trip by train just to see the game.

When the contest, won 22-9 by Army, was over, this fan boarded a train for the arduous return trip home. There were no super-speed Amtrak trains at this time. So it took all night before he arrived in Washington, D.C.

The fan was none other than President Woodrow Wilson. His party included his daughter Eleanor; Joseph P. Tumulty, secretary to the president; Dr. Cary T. Grayson, the White House physician; and the secret service men.

Sure, the president was tired after the long trip back. But he was still flowing with adrenaline. He went straight to the White House to have breakfast with his wife and another daughter Margaret, and regaled them with stories about the exciting football contest he had just witnessed.

He also told them that Mr. and Mrs. Sayre, their daughter and son-in-law, had departed for Europe without a hitch on the Saturday morning of the game.

It was Wilson's custom to attend church on Sunday morning. Not this time. According to the *Washington Post*, "The President did not attend church . . . but rested until shortly after 2 o'clock."

Then he and Mrs. Wilson "took a long automobile ride. They returned to the White House at 5:30."

Somehow, the president managed to also squeeze in over the weekend a conference with the Democratic leaders who were engineering a currency bill in the Senate.

A full weekend, indeed, for President Wilson.

Navy Visionaries

In 1925 there was naturally no TV to broadcast football games. But there was radio, and it was the only way to follow the Army-Navy game if you couldn't attend it in New York.

Well, not the only way.

When naval officers, Midshipmen, and professors who couldn't leave Annapolis gathered in Mahan Hall at the Naval Academy on the day of the game, a number of speakers had been arranged in the room for the broadcast.

There was more than the play by play on radio, though. A miniature football field had been set up and as the game progressed, a Navy man moved a miniature football up and down to give the audience a better "vision" of the game.

The Navy men enjoyed everything but the final score, which ended 10-3 in favor of Army.

All the Marbles

Just because the Army-Navy football series didn't start until 1890 didn't mean that there weren't any strong competitive feelings between the two academies before that.

In 1868, three vessels of the "Naval Academy Practice Squadron" had anchored in the Hudson River, off West Point. The Navy men issued Army a challenge: meet us in either a baseball game or a boat race.

Sorry, the Army boys fired back, there were neither boats nor bats at West Point.

But, wait a minute, the Cadets did have marbles. Plenty of them. In fact, they boasted of having some great marble shooters, some of the best in the East.

Would the Middies like to engage them in a game of marbles?

The Middies reluctantly declined. Unlike Army, good marble shooters were scarce in the Navy. It was obvious that you couldn't very well practice marble shooting on a rolling boat.

The Last Draw

When fans picked up their programs at the Army-Navy game of 1984, they might have been a bit perplexed by the cover.

Instead of the usual Norman Rockwell–type drawings of exaggerated Army generals and Navy admirals that many had grown accustomed to, there was merely the picture of a drawing board with the words, "I give up" scrawled across it.

The message was signed by Gib Crockett, the *Washington Star* cartoonist who had done forty-one years of classic Army-Navy program covers. His latest effort also included a chair with two officers' hats.

In a story inside the program, Crockett gave his reason for not wanting to do Army-Navy program covers anymore: "I don't have any more ideas," he said. "I've been doing it for forty-one years, isn't that enough?"

Asked what he thought fans would think, he replied: "They'll probably think I'm dead, but that's all right."

Perfect Game

In 1957 an Associated Press writer turned in a perfect score on football picks in a contest sponsored by the *Washington Post*.

His reward: two tickets to the Army-Navy game in Philadelphia, plus expenses for two.

Joseph W. Hall Jr. surprised his AP colleagues by running the table on twenty games. After all, he was on the AP's Senate staff, specializing in financial stories, not sports. He admittedly was not a sports expert.

"I suppose I just got lucky," Hall said.

As for the so-called experts, no one in the AP sports bureau could match Hall's score.

Boy, Were They Upset

As the Army-Navy game approaches each year, tremendous stress mounts for each team—particularly the coaches, whose jobs very often depend on the outcome.

However, Eddie Erdelatz didn't show any outward sign of nervousness before the 1950 game as he wisecracked with the press right through the week leading up to the game in Philadelphia.

Maybe it was because not much was expected of Navy, which had won only two of eight games in Erdelatz's first season at the Middies' helm. They were 21-point underdogs to a powerful Army team that had won its first eight games of the season.

Just before the contest, Erdelatz heard that the Cadets were upset because they had been ranked no better than second to Oklahoma in the weekly Associated Press poll.

Talking with reporters, Erdelatz cracked:

"We're burned up, too. We're ranked sixty-five and we should be sixty-four."

By the way, the team with nothing to lose, didn't.

Navy beat Army 14-2 in one of the biggest upsets in the rivalry's history.

Is He Kidding?

Before the 1955 Army-Navy game, Middies coach Eddie Erdelatz expressed some skepticism about a remark by opposing coach Earl Blaik. The Army coach told reporters he only has "five or six players" compared to the depth of the well-balanced Navy team.

Erdelatz, known for his quick-witted remarks, answered Blaik the only way he knew how, with a touch of humor.

"It would sure help us with our planning for Saturday if someone would tell us who the five are on the Army team who are football players," Erdelatz said.

Somehow, Army managed to overcome Blaik's dire pessimism to beat Navy, 14-6.

Not So Cheery

When some 3,300 of their Naval Academy classmates departed for the 1958 Army-Navy game, three "miserable" Midshipmen were left behind to cheer as best they could by proxy.

First classmen Sydney E. Foscato and Charles B. Kretchner and second classman W. B. Curley all were sick and couldn't make the trip from Annapolis to Philadelphia.

The trio remained in sick bay at Bancroft Hall, a Naval Academy dormitory, and heard the game on radio. Foscato and Kretchner seemed to have the worst of it, with catarrhal fever, commonly known as "cat fever." But there was nothing wrong with their voices. When Navy scored first, they shook the near deserted dormitory halls with their cheers.

Except for Curley. The best he could manage was a whisper. He had laryngitis. Not only couldn't Curley go to the game, he couldn't cheer, either.

"This Is Graham McNamee . . ."

Safe to say no other college football game has the far-reaching impact of Army-Navy, with servicemen all over the world tuning in for the action no matter where they are and no matter the time of day.

As far back as the Radio Age, military forces from Europe to Asia could hear the play-by-play, even if in some cases it was slightly delayed because of the distances involved.

In 1930 the broadcast from the stadium was sent by land wire to Annapolis and Arlington, Virginia. And from there it was sent out on short-wave length by the naval wireless stations.

These two high-powered stations broadcast the game directly to Panama, ships in the Caribbean, and to European stations.

"San Francisco picked it up from Annapolis and rebroadcast it to Honolulu, which sent it to Cavito (in the Phillipines)," reported the *New York Times*. "The latter point rebroadcast it to ships of the Asiatic Fleet in Chinese and Japanese waters."

In some cases, the voice of announcer Graham McNamee was heard three to seven minutes behind transmission because of all the relays.

But the servicemen heard it, nevertheless.

Time for a Change?

Before the 1974 Army-Navy game, the top officers at each school made a friendly bet.

Maj. Gen. Sidney B. Berry of West Point and Adm. William P. Mack of the Naval Academy shook hands that the loser would buy the winner a new bathrobe.

For Berry, that would certainly be unique.

"I have an old bathrobe that I've worn since I graduated from West Point in 1948," Berry said. "My wife wants me to buy a new one, but I told her to hold off because I was going to challenge Admiral Mack to a bet and told her I'd be wearing a new robe after November 30."

Unfortunately for Berry's wife, she would have to wait longer than that. Navy beat Army 19-0 that year, then won the next two games in the series to extend its winning streak over Army to four.

No word if Berry ever bought a new bathrobe by then.

Coach Speak

The 1974 Army-Navy game wasn't exactly a Clash of the Titans with both teams entering the contest with 3-7 records. Navy, though, was thought to be a little better—although not quite up to the performance of the previous year when the Middies had stomped Army 51-0 in the biggest rout of the rivalry

"We have been the underdogs this year by as many as 35 points, but I see where we're only a seven-point underdog against Navy," said Army coach Homer Smith. "That's like being a favorite to us."

Navy coach George Welsh had to chuckle at Smith's comments.

"I guess that what Homer is trying to tell you is that I have the better team and if we lose that means he will have out-coached me," Welsh said.

Welsh was also worried that Navy's embarrassment of Army the year before would "come back to haunt me."

No need to worry. As it turned out, Navy still covered the spread by a nice margin by beating the Cadets 19-0.

Rallying the Troops

Freshmen at West Point know all about the Army-Navy football rivalry, sort of. Only after they experience a pregame pep rally do they really *know*.

Achim Biller attended such a rally in the 1990s, expecting some harmless fraternity-type fun.

Guess again.

> Shades of the "Deathmobile" in *Animal House*, a tank rumbled over the top of a pickup truck bearing the Navy insignia. Several Cadets came out of the crowd and completed the demolishing job with sledgehammers.
> A boat labeled "Navy" was turned into a raging bonfire.
> A Blackhawk helicopter roared overhead and Army Rangers came sliding down by rope to the wild cheers of the Cadets.

Then usually conservative West Point superintendent Daniel Christian gave a Knute Rockne–type pep talk and ripped off his shirt in twenty-degree weather to reveal a T-shirt bearing Army's well-known "A" logo.

The Cadets then chanted, "Beat Navy! Beat Navy!"

Recalled Biller: "That gave me an idea of the game's magnitude."

In Bad Taste

You hear the words "Beat Army" just about every day of the year at the Naval Academy. Navy plebes have discovered they are sometimes more than just words.

Once during Army-Navy week leading up to the Big Game, Navy plebes were invited to try out a horrid homemade concoction called the "Beat Army!" The recipe that particular year featured ketchup, Jell-O, peanut butter, salt, pepper, and salad dressing.

"It wasn't too good," recalled one Navy man, swallowing his pride along with the other stuff.

He kept a stiff upper lip, though. "It was fun to know I was part of the tradition."

Time Out for a Celebration

It was late at night on December 3, 1944, near Leyte in the Phillipines. Lt. Gen. Robert Eichelberger put aside the war for a few hours to listen to the Army-Navy game being broadcast over Armed Forces Radio from Baltimore.

When the game ended at 2 A.M., Eichelberger jumped into a jeep with some fellow officers and took off like a shot. Risking life and limb, he drove through a raging tropical downpour. Finally, Eichelberger and his companions arrived at the front to seek out Col. Charles "Monk" Meyer, an all-American quarterback who played on Army's 1935 team.

They trudged through muck and mire before finding Meyer. The officers all lifted a toast to Doc Blanchard and Glenn Davis and the great Army team that had just beaten Navy, 23-7.

Then Eichelberger and his companions drove back to their camp to continue the war.

Signing Off

The Army-Navy game brings out the best in both academies, and not only the football players.

Each year the students seem to come up with more creative

ideas to poke fun at each other. One year when Army was being criticized for a light schedule, the Midshipmen sang the following parody of the famed West Point song, "On, Brave Old Army Team":

> We don't play Notre Dame,
> We don't play Tulane,
> But we play Davidson,
> For that's the fearless Army team.

The Midshipmen unfurled a banner that said, "When do you drop Navy?"

The Cadets, who had somehow gotten wind of the Navy plans to mock them, answered with a sign of their own. "Today!" it said.

Not to be outdone, Navy came back with: "Why not schedule Vassar?"

Army responded with another sign: "We already got Navy!"

Keeping Up

John McCain spent five and a half years in a North Vietnamese prison camp after his plane was shot down over Hanoi. News from the States was scarce, so McCain counted on new prisoners to update him whenever they came in.

McCain, a former Navy pilot and now United States senator from Arizona, was interested, of course, in how the war was going, among other things.

Before asking that compelling question, though, he usually wanted to know just one thing first: "Who won last year's Army-Navy game?"

Field Expediency

American servicemen stationed around the world will go to great lengths to keep in touch with the Army-Navy game. One officer in Hong Kong took a radio to his room with the intention of listening to the play-by-play over Armed Forces Radio. But the connection wouldn't fit and he was unable to plug it in.

What to do?

The officer wound up getting game reports via his walkie-talkie to his ship in the harbor.

A Mind Game

For one group of American prisoners of war in Vietnam, the Army-Navy game might be called a life-saver. If anything, it probably saved their sanity.

Cdr. Jack Fellows, a 1956 graduate of the Naval Academy, was a prisoner of war for six years and seven months at the Zoo Prison near Hanoi. It didn't stop Fellows and the other Americans from holding "an Army-Navy weekend each year."

"We'd tap on the wall that everyone should come over to a certain room for make-believe beer and pretzels," Fellows said. "And would we dream up magnificent menus for the postgame celebrations!"

Those special "Army-Navy weekends" helped keep spirits up during the Americans' long internment. Fellows said he even made "bets" with Air Force men who were graduates of West Point.

"We'd tap fake scores to each other through the wall," he said. "The one who got the first tap in usually was the winner."

If at First . . .

Talk about the best laid plans . . .

One year the Cadets constructed a giant wooden cannon, from which they intended to shoot a dummy sailor clear across the field at the Army-Navy game.

First they test-fired it on their own parade grounds and sent the "sailor" sailing five hundred feet. Too far, the Cadets figured. They didn't want the thing to travel clear out of the football field, 100,000-seat Municipal Stadium in Philadelphia, only across the field.

So they reduced the powder charge to more proper proportions and sent the cannon off to Municipal Stadium.

It never got inside, however. While reducing the powder charge, the Cadets forgot to reduce the size of the cannon. It was too big to fit through any of the entrances.

It didn't deter the Cadets the next year, though. This time, they sent a smaller cannon to the game, and got it inside the stadium. And this time, they got their shot at Navy.

Of Mules and Goats

Who came first, the goat or the mule?

Navy is the winner in this game of one-upmanship, and it isn't even close.

The goat made its appearance at the very first Army-Navy game in 1890. The Middies saw the creature on their march from the ferry station at Highland Falls to the Plains at West Point, and whimsically shanghaied the goat for a mascot.

The mule became the Army mascot several years later when an officer at the Philadelphia Quartermaster Depot decided that the Cadets needed something to counteract the Navy goat.

The choice of a mule generally reflected the long-standing usefulness of the creature in military operations, such as hauling ammunition, guns, and supplies.

The first Army mascot, though, actually pulled an ice wagon.

Getting Navy's Goat . . . and Army's Mule

Stunts involving the mascots have become a part of the Army-Navy tradition—and each school has come up with creative ways to showcase its own.

At one Army-Navy game, the goat came on the field in a float designed as a perfume bottle. In another, the goat came out of a Trojan horse.

The Navy goat takes a moment to speak with the press.
Courtesy of the United States Military Academy

As for Army, before one service clash a pair of mules rode on a trailer truck billed as "Army's Answer to Atomic Warfare." Needless to say, the Middies were delighted when the truck got stuck in the mud near one of the end zones.

In the past, kidnapping the goat before the Army-Navy game was a high priority at West Point. Same for Navy and the mule. This practice has since been outlawed by the academies.

In 1989 a posse of Middies kidnapped three Army mule mascots and high-tailed it back to Annapolis, where they presented them at their pregame rally.

One year a "goatnapping" resulted in this ad in the *New York Times*: "Hey, Navy! Do you know where your 'kid' is today? The Corps does."

Another time, after the Cadets kidnapped the goat, they sent the animal back with a military escort commanded by a colonel professing some regret. Said the colonel upon his arrival at the Naval Academy: "They say in the Army there are four general classes of officers—aides, aviators, asses, or adjutants. I am adjutant at West Point, have been playing aide to a goat all day, and feel like a bit of an ass."

Ghost Story

One night before the Army-Navy game in 1972, Cadets swore they had seen the apparition of a cavalry soldier from the 1830s. There was also a frightening chill in the barracks when the apparition appeared. A ghost?

No, a prank.

Midshipman William Gravell ultimately came forth to confess that the "apparition" was nothing more than a trick involving a flashlight, photographic slide, and a fire extinguisher.

What the Cadets had seen in their half-awake state in the

middle of the night was the slide of a Midshipman dressed in bits and pieces of an old uniform projected against the wall. The chill felt by the Cadets? Just the fire extinguisher producing carbon dioxide, that's all.

Dust to Dust

Think abuse is rampant at Army-Navy games as the Cadets and Middies try to put down each other?

Imagine being the exchange officer who is stationed at the opposite Academy.

A number of horror stories involving these luckless military men have surfaced over the years. Here are just a couple:

While stationed at the Naval Academy, Maj. Charles Wuerple came back to his room to find it painted Navy blue and gold. That wasn't the worst. Another time he was locked in his room with a mule that had been fed Ex-Lax™. And then there was the time the Middies took his car to the mess hall and had it filled with cereal.

In 1969 another Army officer didn't think Annapolis was too much fun, either, when the Middies surrounded his house one night and announced they were going to demolish his car with sledgehammers. As he looked on in shock and horror, the officer watched the Middies whack away at his vehicle until it was nearly dust.

P.S.: This story had a happy ending. The Navy men had each chipped in enough money to hand the officer a check for $4,000, enough to replace his old car with a new one.

But for a while there, *gotcha!*

Ear-Splitting

They've been called the "Rabble Rousers," and the Cadets cheerleaders usually live up to the nickname.

One year at an Army-Navy game they distributed air horns and tin clickers, which sounded like crickets, to the thousands of Cadets in the stands.

"Those 8,000 clickers (two per man) made some racket," said one fan who sat near the Army section that day. "Then the air horns joined in, and there really was some noise."

Like they needed any more noise for an Army-Navy game.

Destroying Graffiti

When it comes to the devious minds of Army and Navy pranksters, nothing's sacred—not even the Navy's most formidable ships.

One year the Navy had a destroyer anchored in the Hudson River opposite the Military Academy. It was ripe for the taking, as far as the Cadets were concerned.

A group of them rowed out to the vessel under the cover of darkness and painted "Beat Navy" on the side of the ship. The Cadets were so enamored of their handiwork, they just had to go out and look at it in daylight the next day.

Big mistake.

The Cadets were "captured" by the crew and forced to clean up their unappreciated artwork.

A Lot of Bull

In 1903 Navy fullback William F. Halsey was having a tough day in the Army-Navy game. His particular nemesis on this day was Army right guard Charles Thompson, who was giving Halsey one of the worst poundings of his football career.

They met many years later, when "Bull" Halsey was an admiral in charge of United States forces in the South Pacific in the Second World War, and Thompson was a major general in the Army.

Halsey didn't pull rank, but did show Thompson he had a long memory.

"General," Halsey said, "the last time I saw you, you were rubbing my nose all over Franklin Field in Philadelphia."

"Admiral," responded Thompson, "how did I know you were going to be my boss in the South Pacific?"

Can You Beat That?

It was 1965, a couple of weeks after Army and Navy had played to a 7-7 tie, and four years before the moon landing. The world looked skyward for a historic rendezvous in space.

Gemini 7 was about to hook up with *Gemini 6*.

Astronauts James Lovell and Frank Borman were in the *Gemini 7* spacecraft and Wally Schirra and Tom Stafford were in *Gemini 6*. Schirra, Stafford, and Borman had attended Annapolis.

Lovell was the only one of the four from West Point.

Slowly *Gemini 7* moved closer to *Gemini 6*. Now the spacecrafts were just a foot apart.

The tension was unbearable.

Borman looked out one of the spacecraft's windows. He told Lovell to take a look, too.

The West Pointer did, and saw a blue and gold sign posted on the window of the *Gemini 6* craft. It said:

"BEAT ARMY."

What could Lovell do? He was up in the air.

Just Kid-ing

It's usually two or three mules on the Cadets' sideline during an Army-Navy game. For the Navy, generally one goat.

One year the Middies had two. Asked why the extra mascot for Navy that day, Middies coach Charlie Weatherbie quipped: "We're deep at goat."

Oh, Brother!

Army-Navy games are generally regarded as brother against brother. Sometimes that is literally true.

The 1926 game matched Chuck Born against his brother, Arthur. Chuck had been a star end on the Army team for three years while Arthur had just established himself as a starting guard on the Navy team that season.

The parents of the Born brothers, from Racine, Wisconsin, attended the game in Chicago. Although they sat on the Army side of the field, they must have had a tough time figuring out who to root for.

How relieved Mr. and Mrs. Born must have felt when the game ended in a 21-21 tie.

Presidential Souvenir

In his senior season in 1948, Bill Yeoman was Army's team captain and a second-team all-American center.

At the Army-Navy game that year, Yeoman won the coin toss (flipped by President Harry Truman) to decide which side kept the ball in the event of a tie.

So when the game ended 21-21, Yeoman figured he'd at least retain the ball for the Cadets' showcase.

"Then I read in the paper that 'The Old Man' had liberated the ball from my room," Yeoman said.

Yeoman didn't go empty-handed, though. Truman sent him

a letter congratulating him on his sportsmanship, and Yeoman still had that letter in a frame many years later.

Unbalanced Line

Carl Ullrich viewed the Army-Navy game from a unique perspective—he was on both sides of the rivalry. Ullrich was assistant athletic director at Navy from 1968–1979 and athletic director at Army from 1980–1985.

"I went through the same negative situation twice," Ullrich once told a reporter. "When I was at the Naval Academy, they were asking why we couldn't beat Army. When I was at Army, they asked the same thing."

Ullrich actually was not a graduate of either school, but had two sons and two sons-in-law who were Naval Academy graduates. How was the loyalty divided in the family?

"They rooted for Navy," Ullrich said.

Just to balance things in the family, Ullrich rooted for Army after he left the Military Academy.

Charlie's Vow

When Army lost to Navy 19-14 in 1967, Charlie Jarvis blamed himself for the Cadets' defeat. With the Cadets driving to go ahead, Jarvis fumbled on Navy's 23-yard line with four minutes left. The Middies recovered and ran out the clock.

The 1968 game was a little different for Jarvis, then a senior. He scored three touchdowns to lead Army's 21-14 victory over Navy.

"He felt personally responsible for the loss in 1967," said Bob Kinney, former sports information director at Army. "He told me he had made a vow to himself never to fumble again, and he never fumbled in his senior year."

Trade Embargo

There was apparently no love lost between Army coach Earl Blaik and Navy coach Eddie Erdlatz during their fierce rivalry in the 1950s. They wouldn't even exchange films before their teams met, according to longtime Navy scout Steve Belichick.

"The schools started trading films in 1959 for the first time," Belichick said. "Prior to that, they didn't trade anything.

"Eddie Erdlatz and Earl Blaik wouldn't give each other the time of day. But Wayne Hardin (of Navy) and Dale Hall (of Army) started the direct exchange, and every coach has done that since."

Down and Out

With usually 100,000 fans present at the Army-Navy game in old Municipal Stadium in Philadelphia, you can imagine the wide variety of articles left behind after the final gun.

After the 1949 game, for instance, Pinkerton police found thirty-one overshoes and a large number of women's earrings. The shoes and earrings were mostly single. In 1950 the police found two filled five-gallon gasoline tanks, whose presence was never explained.

One time the Pinkerton report told of an incoherent woman found in the men's room. She had been asleep for several hours after the game. When asked for her identity, the woman was totally clueless. She could give neither her name, address, nor any information about the people she was with.

She was taken away in a radio car to await identification.

"Seemed intoxicated," the Pinkerton report said with some caution.

Goes Better with Milk

Shortly before the 1967 Army-Navy game, some of the Cadets gave the Middies billboard material that fired them up.

One Army player was quoted as saying Navy quarterback John Cartwright "rattles under pressure." Another told a reporter he "was not impressed with the Navy pass defense."

Army had an 8-1 record and was a 6 ½-point favorite over Navy, which was 4-4-1.

So guess what?

Cartwright led the Middies to a 17-0 halftime lead, engineering a magnificent 93-yard drive for one of the touchdowns, and had one of the best games of his career. Meanwhile, Navy's "unimpressive" pass defense only allowed one touchdown toss late in the game and the Middies walked off with a 19-14 upset of the Cadets.

The Middies then celebrated in the dressing room by showering each other with milk.

Cartwright finished off a brilliant season by breaking six of Roger Staubach's Navy records. After the game he told reporters he had kept Army's demeaning remarks "up here," pointing to his forehead.

As if he needed more incentive to beat Army.

Imagine That

Navy halfback Joe Bellino had a hard time going to sleep the night before the 1959 game with Army. He comforted himself with this scene:

He imagined that a gaping hole opened on the Army line and he rushed through, faked out Army halfback Bob Anderson, and raced into the end zone. He kept replaying that scene in his mind, like watching the Navy goat jump a fence, until he finally fell asleep.

Now it was game day and Navy was on offense. Quarterback Joe Tranchini handed the ball off to Bellino. He bolted through an opening in the middle of the line, cut to the right and before the startled Anderson could reach him, the Middies' running back was past him and on his way to the end zone.

He told reporters after the game it was almost the way he had imagined it the night before.

P.S.: Navy won 43-12 as Bellino scored three touchdowns. It was the first time in the Army-Navy rivalry that a player scored three touchdowns. That was probably something that not even the cocky Bellino could imagine.

Certainly Not at a Loss for Words

During Navy's sorrowful 1959 season, the Middies were having a hard time scoring points. After a while, coach Rick Forzano could only joke about it.

"We couldn't make a first down running against a strong wind," he quipped.

After a 47-0 beating by Notre Dame, Forzano said with a grin: "When Notre Dame put the women and children in there against us in the fourth quarter, it was pretty embarrassing."

Not surprisingly, one of Navy's worst teams was beaten 27-0 by Army to mercifully end the Middies season at 1-9. As Army tried to run out the clock in the final minute, fans came pouring out of the stands to tear down the goalposts.

"What do we do now?" one Army player asked a referee.

"Just finish the game," the official said. "Don't try to kick any field goals."

Sleepless in Princeton

In the early days of the Army-Navy rivalry, one of the games was played at Princeton.

Apparently one was enough.

About a month before the start of the 1911 season, no contract had yet been worked out to return the game to the University of Pennsylvania's Franklin Field.

Rumors were rampant the game would return to Princeton for that season, according to the *Washington Post*. This was strongly denied by Navy.

"Naval men have branded as absolutely without foundation the declaration that the army-navy [sic] football game this fall would be held at the Princeton oval," the *Post* said in a story datelined from Philadelphia on August 11, 1930.

The reason? The academies had no desire to return to Princeton following a disastrous experience there in 1905.

"In discussing the Princeton story, navy [sic] men here call attention to the 1905 game when many of the followers of the flag went hungry because Princeton was unable to feed them, and more went sleepless because the college town could not house them," the *Post* reported. "They also recall it was two days before the limited railroad facilities in the little town were able to move the rear guard and allow them to return to their homes."

Good reason for the Army-Navy game to return to Philadelphia, which it did in 1911. From then on it was played in big venues, except for a couple of years during the Second World War when it returned to the schools' respective campuses.

So Near, Yet So Far

It's not like being there, but American troops in Iraq still find it fun to watch the Army-Navy game. And the United States military tries to make it fun for them.

During a recent Army-Navy game, soldiers at Champion Base in Ar Ramadi gathered to watch a tape delay broadcast of the game.

The military commanders spared no expense. They flew in the 82nd Airborne Division's band to play before the game. And there was a big tailgate party, with barbecue pits.

The only thing missing was the beer. Under "General Order Number One," alcohol has been outlawed.

The troops could drink "near-beer," of course. And eat "near pizza," a concoction in pita bread that one soldier called "not even close to the real thing."

It was obvious that the troops were not happy with "General Order Number One," although some managed to keep their sense of humor about it.

"At least we're allowed to have near-fun," said one soldier.

16

CLASSIC GAMES

How do you figure?

A team with only two victories all season beats a team ranked No. 2 in the country and riding a twenty-eight-game unbeaten streak.

How do you figure?

A team with the nation's top offense loses when it is stopped cold at the goal line in the fourth quarter.

How do you figure?

A quarterback out of position fails to complete a pass, but still leads his team to victory.

Figure Army-Navy.

Three games within a six-year period of the 1950s provided some of the most gripping battles and most surprising moments in the history of the rivalry.

1950

It was the beginning of the Eddie Erdelatz coaching era at Navy and he was struggling in his first season. The Middies had gone 2-6, losing by scores such as 30-7 to Pennsylvania and 27-0 to Tulane.

Army, meanwhile, was riding high under the savvy, experienced coaching of Earl "Red" Blaik. The Cadets had won their first eight games, including five shutouts. They continued an unbeaten streak that started in 1947 and included a 38-0 rout of Navy in 1949.

The Cadets were ranked No. 2 in the country. Blaik thought they deserved to be No. 1, a view shared by more than a few. He expressed his indignation on the eve of the Navy game.

Upon hearing this, an amused Erdelatz quipped: "We're burned up, too. We're ranked sixty-five and we should be sixty-fourth."

All kidding aside, it was generally believed it would take a great team effort by Navy to win. And even then, the oddsmakers weren't sure: They made the Middies 21-point underdogs.

But the Middies themselves didn't feel like underdogs. They had extra motivation: Navy hadn't beaten Army since 1943. They went into the game with the intent of a victim desperately wanting to turn around the succession of beatings at the hands of the Cadets.

But a crowd of 101,000 at Philadelphia's Municipal Stadium, including President Harry Truman, expected the worst for Navy—particularly after the Middies fumbled away the ball on their 22-yard line in the early going.

The Middies raised eyebrows when they stopped the Cadets on four straight downs. Another surprise: When the Middies had their own similar opportunity in the second period, they cashed in.

They recovered a fumble on the Army 27, and in just four plays, quarterback Bob "Zug" Zastrow led Navy to a score. Zastrow carried seven yards through the middle to cap the drive.

Later in the period, the Middies needed just five plays to go sixty-three yards for another score. Zastrow threw a 30-yard touchdown pass to Jim Baldinger against an Army defense that had allowed but four touchdowns in its previous eight games.

At the half, the Middies had a 14-0 lead. Even more surprising, they had held the Cadets to merely one first down and three yards rushing. They had averaged 312 in their first eight contests.

The second half wasn't much better for the Cadets as the ferocious Navy defense continued to apply the kind of pressure they hadn't faced all season.

"Army's . . . usually smooth speed out of the huddle, designed to get the jump on unwary opponents, gradually deteriorated into a frantic haste," reported *Newsweek*. "The Middies were always dug in and waiting."

The Cadets finally scored in the third period when they tackled Zastrow behind the goal line for a safety, cutting Navy's lead to 14-2.

But Army's high-powered offense was unable to do anything. Seven times the Cadets drove inside Navy's 20-yard line in the second half, only to be turned back by the determined Middies' defense.

All told, Navy had almost as many interceptions (five) as Army had completions (six in twenty-four attempts).

And Navy pulled off a 14-2 upset that Erdelatz called "the greatest team effort I've ever seen."

Blaik was almost too stunned to speak.

"We were well-scouted offensively," was about all he could manage.

Then, alluding to the hard-to-quantify spirit always present in Army-Navy affairs, he added: "They out-charged us . . . they overwhelmed us."

1954

By 1954, the Middies were no longer huge underdogs in the Army-Navy game. In fact, they were considered just about the equals of the Cadets. It would be Navy's top-rated defense against Army's No. 1 offense in a classic battle for Eastern supremacy. A major bowl bid was just about certain for the winner.

The only similarity to 1950 was that Erdelatz was still making tongue-in-cheek observations. The day before the game, Erdelatz remarked that Army "should win by six points."

Blaik didn't believe Erdelatz's sentiments for a minute.

"Maybe Erdelatz knows, but I don't," Blaik said. "I'm not a seer. It will be settled on this (Municipal Stadium) field tomorrow."

If you believe the results of the "Goats-Engineers" game, Army had a better than average chance of winning.

At Army, the "Goats" were the bottom 10 percent of the junior class and the "Engineers" were in the top 10 percent. It had become a tradition every Thanksgiving morning for them to play a friendly football game.

Tradition held that when the Goats beat the Engineers, Army beat Navy 60 percent of the time. So there was a lot of celebrating in 1954 on the West Point campus when the Goats beat the Engineers 6-0.

Meanwhile, the Middies were planning to celebrate in a different way—by dunking their coaches after the final practice. If they could catch them, that is. Erdelatz and his staff managed to evade the tradition the previous two years.

But when the final football exercise was completed on Farragut Field, the Navy coaches found themselves escorted to the pool in Macdonough Hall. Then they found themselves pushed into the pool for an unscheduled bath.

Erdlatz explained how he had escaped the tradition before: "Two years ago, we wound up practice with wind sprints, and when the players were heading downfield we beat it out the other way. Last year, we sent them around the field and ducked through a hole in the fence into my car, which had been standing there with the motor running all through practice."

Just before the game, Army rolled out a prodigious float, described by one writer as "a massive truck that was as big as a couple of moving vans." On the side, the inscription: "Army's answer to atomic warfare."

But, to the vast embarrassment of the Cadets, the float was suddenly bogged down in a section of mud. The Midshipmen hooted in delight until the float was finally pushed free.

Then, there was football to play.

The matchup of Army, No. 5 in the national polls, against No. 6 Navy was expected to be memorable. And it lived up to expectations with a number of lead changes, rallies, and counterrallies.

Navy took a 14-6 lead midway through the first half.

Back came Army.

The Cadets' Don Holleder pounced on a fumble at Navy's 3-yard line and Pat Uebel slashed over the goal line. The extra point cut Navy's lead to 14-13.

Not long after, quarterback Pete Vann threw a 42-yard touchdown pass to Paul Kyasky to give Army the lead, 20-14.

Back came Navy.

Starting at midfield, George Welsh moved Navy downfield and the quarterback finished the drive with a 5-yard run. With an extra point, Navy took back the lead, 21-20.

Whew! All within the first half.

In the second, the Middies drove to Army's 9-yard line, only to lose the ball on a fumble. The Cadets were forced to punt. This time, the Middies didn't waste their chance. Welsh threw a touchdown pass to Earle Smith for a 27-20 lead.

Game over? Not yet.

Army drove to the Navy 8-yard line late in the game, but the Middies turned back the Cadets to seal the victory and send them to the Sugar Bowl.

Erdelatz had dubbed this squad "A Team Named Desire," and it certainly seemed to fit.

"I don't want to sound like a broken record," the Navy coach said, "but desire won this game for us."

1955

Could desire win for Army in 1955, when the Cadets played the role of underdogs? After all, Navy had George Welsh and Army had "Blaik's Folly."

That was what journalists and fans were calling Blaik's dramatic decision to move end Holleder to quarterback at the start of the season. Blaik didn't have anyone else with experience for that critical position, he said. Holleder, who had never played quarterback, reluctantly agreed to the switch.

By the time the Cadets got to the Navy game, they had a 5-3 record. But even though Holleder had improved as a quarterback throughout the season, he certainly wasn't considered in the class of Welsh, one of the country's top quarterbacks.

As expected in the 1955 meeting, Welsh quickly put Navy on the scoreboard with a touchdown drive on the very first possession. The quarterback dashed the final yard to give Navy a 6-0 lead at the half.

Then something unexpected happened. Disdaining the passing game, Holleder brought the Cadets back with a fierce ground game.

In the third period, Army took a 7-6 lead on a touchdown run by Uebel. Then the Cadets made it 14-6 in the fourth quarter on a 22-yard run by Peter Lash.

Even though Welsh's pinpoint aerial game kept Navy moving downfield, the Middies simply could not push over a score.

And Holleder, who tried only two passes all afternoon and completed neither of them, directed the Cadets to a 14-6 victory. The Cadets made all of their 283 yards on the ground under the expert guidance of Holleder.

It turned out "Blaik's Folly" wasn't any folly at all.

1963

Many great football games are remembered for special moments, special plays, or Hollywood endings. The 1963 Army-Navy game is most remembered for a play that never happened. For an improbable script. And for an imperfect ending that haunted the losers and humbled the winners.

The game had been postponed for a week because of the assassination of President Kennedy on November 22. It was rescheduled for December 7, coincidentally another dark date in United States history.

The Middies were ranked No. 2 in the country, with only one close loss to SMU in their first nine games, and were favored by eleven points. Led by quarterback Roger Staubach, the Heisman Trophy winner, Navy had beaten such highly regarded teams as Michigan and Notre Dame on the road.

But the Middies still had to beat Army to gain a Cotton Bowl berth against top-ranked Texas that would create a national championship matchup. Otherwise, Army would go to Dallas despite two losses that included a 28-0 pounding by Pitt, a team Navy had beaten by twelve points.

The difference in coaching approaches made this service clash even more intriguing. It was Wayne Hardin's wide-open, razzle-dazzle style for Navy versus Paul Dietzel's more conservative approach at Army.

In the matchup of quarterbacks, there seemed to be no contest. The Middies had a Heisman Trophy winner and the Cadets had a kid named Rollie Stichweh, a converted halfback and more of a runner than a passer.

So you could hardly blame Hardin for being fairly confident.

"We think we are the No. 1 team in the nation," he said. "We want to prove it."

But this was Army-Navy, where records rarely mean a thing.

"Don't panic," Dietzel mockingly told his Army team.

The Cadets didn't need any bulletin-board material to get psyched for this game. It wasn't just that the Cotton Bowl was at stake. Army was looking for revenge after losing four straight games to Navy. The Middies emphasized that point when they came on the field with "Drive for Five" lettered on the back of their gold uniforms.

From the opening kickoff, this was a special Army-Navy encounter.

Scouting from the press box, Texas coach Darrell Royal observed: "I'll tell you one thing. Nobody's backing off down there. They're trying to maim each other."

At first, it was Army doing most of the "maiming."

Stichweh (rhymes with "which way") had Army going the right way on its first possession. He moved the Cadets sixty-five yards, capping the drive with a touchdown run from the 10.

Rollie Stichweh.
Courtesy of the United States Military Academy

Staubach then showed why he won the Heisman. He directed touchdown drives of forty-seven, eighty, and ninety-one yards, each time sending fullback Pat Donnelly over for the score.

So with 10:32 remaining, Navy had what looked like a safe 21-7 lead.

Then Stichweh started to look like Staubach.

He moved the Cadets to a quick touchdown with the help of the running of halfback Ken Waldrop and a smart game plan. When Navy stacked its defense on the flanks, Stichweh sent Waldrop smashing over tackle for big chunks of yardage. When the Middies stacked up the middle, Stichweh scampered around the ends.

Stichweh capped the drive when he rolled to his right from the Navy 5 and leaped into the end zone. Then he added the two-point conversion with another rollout, cutting Navy's lead to 21-15.

Ho hum, just another Army-Navy barnburner.

But no one could have figured the way this one was going to end.

"They're going to try an onside kick just as soon as the referee gives them the ball," Royal mused in the press box.

An onside kick, it was. And guess who recovered: none other than the ubiquitous Stichweh.

Now Army had the ball back with 6:13 to go. And the Cadets were on the Navy 49-yard line. Good field position and seemingly plenty of time for the Cadets to beat Navy for the first time since 1958.

"SMU AND ARMY, TOO," chanted the Cadets in the stands, reminding Navy of its 32-28 loss at Southern Methodist that season.

Another Navy loss seemed probable as Stichweh methodically moved Army down the field. But Army needed to hurry up. Out of timeouts, the Cadets had used up a good bit of the clock while clawing out three first downs.

With 1:38 to go, the Cadets had a first down on the Navy 7-yard line.

"TOUCHDOWN! TOUCHDOWN!" the corps of Cadets screamed.

"STOP THEM! STOP THEM!" Navy rooters answered.

Navy could not. But something else could.

Don Parcells gained two yards, Waldrop got one, then Waldrop got two more.

The Navy players deliberately took their time getting untangled from the mass pileup on the last play.

"I was underneath all of it," said Navy tackle Jim Freeman, "but I had sort of a peephole to look at the clock. I was in no hurry to get up."

"I don't think any Navy player was in a hurry to get up," added Navy guard Alex Krekich.

Now it was fourth down and two yards to go for a touchdown. A winning touchdown.

Sixteen seconds left.

One final try for the game winner—if Army could get off the play.

The din of the 102,000 fans was overwhelming, so much so that before each of those plays approaching the Navy goal line, Stichweh asked referee Barney Finn to stop the clock to quiet the crowd. Stichweh's teammates couldn't hear his signals. As a result, the Army team had lost precious seconds off the clock.

"Near the end of the game, the excitement level, the noise level was incredible," Stichweh remembered in an interview many years later. "It was bedlam."

Banners and streamers were flying around in a stiff December wind at venerable Municipal Stadium. Roaring fans had already started spilling onto the field in the back of the end zone when Stichweh brought the Army team to the line for one last try at the Navy goal line. The scene was surrealistic.

Too much noise again. And again, Stichweh asked Finn to stop the clock. Finn complied.

Unwisely, Stichweh brought his team back for another huddle. He and his teammates were unaware that the clock had only been stopped momentarily, and it restarted while they were huddling.

By the time they started back to the line of scrimmage for the fourth-down play, the Cadets could not believe their eyes. They looked on in shocked disbelief as the referee picked up the ball and declared the game over.

Navy 21, Army 15.

Time just ran out on Army.

Staubach had been watching nervously from the sideline as the final minutes of the drama unfolded.

"I must have said a hundred Hail Marys," he said later.

Hardin also issued a sigh of relief.

"I feel awful humble," the Navy coach said. "You just can't crow over a game like this."

And Army felt saddened and speechless. The Cadets had to be thinking what might have been if only for a few seconds more.

"Although Navy clearly was happy to squeak away with the victory, there were regrets on both sides that the players were not the ones to decide the game," Stitchweh said. "I do regret not having the opportunity for one more play. It would have been fun to see what the outcome would have been."

17

SIDELINE STRATEGISTS

America's outstanding military academies have, appropriately, been led onto the football field by some brilliant coaches. The two who stand out most are Hall of Famers: Earl Blaik of Army and George Welsh of Navy.

Earl Blaik

Argue all you want about the greatest player in Army-Navy history. Choose one all-American or another, one Heisman Trophy winner or another.

But there can be little disagreement who was the best coach at either academy.

Earl "Red" Blaik won three national championships, seven Lambert Trophies, and 121 of the 164 games he coached. He guided the Black Knights of the Hudson to two perfect seasons and three in which they had no losses, but were tied. From

1944–1946, Army won twenty-five straight games and in a six-year span, the Cadets went 57-3-3.

"No one will ever think of Army football without thinking of Col. Red Blaik," said former West Point superintendent Lt. Gen. Dave R. Palmer. "His name is synonymous with excellence in Army athletics."

Yet against the Naval Academy, Blaik went a mere 8-8-2. The man that one West Point official once saw on campus and "expected to walk across Lusk Reservoir" had his most trouble with his biggest rival.

What does that say about the intensity and importance of each Army-Navy game? Through Army's golden era, Blaik left the big game a winner only half the time.

In a strange way, that might have been fitting.

"If it is the game most like war," Blaik said, "it is also the most like life, for it teaches young men that work, sacrifice, selflessness, competitive drive, perseverance, and respect for authority are the price one pays to achieve goals worthwhile."

That, naturally, goes for players wearing Navy blue as much as Army gray.

In his first three matchups with Navy, Blaik not only couldn't guide the Cadets to victory, but his teams managed a total of six points in those contests. Yes, he had turned around a floundering program (1-7-1 in 1940) with winning records in 1941, 1942, and 1943, but Blaik had not beaten Navy. Hardly even scored on the Middies.

The first of those three losses came against Maj. Emory "Swede" Larson, who was 3-0 as a player and 3-0 as a coach against Army.

"This game is different from all the rest," Blaik admitted. "And if you lose, you have a whole winter to think about it."

Of course, these were the war years—Blaik's first Army-

Navy game occurred a week before Pearl Harbor was attacked by the Japanese.

The 1942 defeat came at Annapolis. President Roosevelt, citing security concerns, ordered the site switched and allowed only the Brigade, the Army team and its support staff, the media, and residents within 10 miles of Annapolis to attend. Although less than 12,000 people showed up, Blaik noted that half of the Middies were ordered to cheer for Army that day.

"It was a strange day, to say the very least," Blaik said of the 14-0 loss.

And it was nearly as strange in 1943, when the game was played at West Point, again because of travel restrictions. And Navy won again, 13-0, "rooted to victory" by designated Cadets, of course.

With an 18-8-2 record, Blaik should have been hailed by soldiers everywhere. Ah, but he was 0-3 versus Navy and that, the coach said, "must change."

In 1944, Blaik, the first noncareer officer to coach Army, finally got his first win over the Midshipmen. It might have been the most memorable in the great coach's career, a 23-7 win that capped an unbeaten season that earned Army the national championship. That victory, sparked by the nonpareil backfield tandem of Doc Blanchard and Glenn Davis, prompted Gen. Douglas MacArthur to send Blaik the following telegram: "THE GREATEST OF ALL ARMY TEAMS. STOP. WE HAVE STOPPED THE WAR TO CELEBRATE YOUR MAGNIFICENT SUCCESS. MACARTHUR."

Blaik was so thrilled with the triumph that he handed out booklets to team members after the season, with a message inscribed:

"Seldom in a lifetime's experience is one permitted the complete satisfaction of being part of a perfect performance. To all the coaches, the 23-7 is enough."

If Blanchard and Davis were "Mr. Inside" and "Mr. Outside," then Blaik was "Coach Everywhere." He was involved in every aspect of Army football, after playing football, baseball, and basketball as a cadet. His players swore that Blaik knew everything that went on in their lives.

"He was genuinely interested in every player he ever had," said Joe Steffy, an all-America guard in 1947. "He was more interested in the third-string guard that didn't graduate than he was in Glenn Davis or Doc Blanchard. Davis and Blanchard could take care of themselves."

One cadet who didn't quite take care of himself properly was Blaik's son, Robert, who was involved in the cheating scandal of 1951 that almost brought down the entire Army athletic program. One of thirty-seven players lost in the scandal, Robert Blaik's participation was only tangential. Young Blaik, a quarterback in 1949 and 1950, had knowledge of cadets passing around test information and did not report it.

His heart-broken father was ready to quit in 1951, believing the dismissal of ninety cadets was far too strict a punishment for the offenses committed by a majority of them, including his son. Others disagreed, with members of the United States Senate calling for a ban on football at the academies.

Blaik had instructed his team leaders to make sure all of his players—indeed all of the Cadets involved in the "cribbing," or passing on information through the corps that could be on tests—came clean. But he knew where such a course was headed, and Blaik determined it was in the best interest of the academy and the football program that he resign.

But Blaik was convinced to stay by perhaps the only person with enough influence on him to do so: his mentor, MacArthur.

"Earl, you must stay on," MacArthur told him. "Don't leave under fire."

He didn't, but it would be 1953 before he would lead Army to a winning record—and a victory over Navy—again.

That year, Blaik was chosen coach of the year by the Touchdown Club of Washington, D.C., as the Cadets went 7-1-1 and beat Navy 20-7.

By the mid-1950s, Blaik was drawing criticism for a weak schedule. Indeed, his opening-game record was 16-2, with 11 shutouts, and in 1955 the Cadets routed Furman 81-0. Blaik, who once coached at Dartmouth, believed playing inferior teams built up confidence and morale.

Blaik's last team was also one of his greatest. The 1958 edition went 8-0-1, tying Pittsburgh 14-14. Led by team captain Pete Dawkins, who would win the Heisman Trophy, the Cadets defeated Navy 22-6 in Blaik's final game at the helm.

"He took me from a raggedly little kid and made of me everything that happened good to me in my career of football," Dawkins said of Blaik.

A close observer and frequent adviser to Army football in his later years, Blaik was awarded the Presidential Medal of Freedom in 1986 by Ronald Reagan. He knew other presidents well and Gerald Ford once told of a letter he received from Blaik.

"Dear Mr. President," Blaik wrote, "do you really think you're furnishing the leadership this country needs, or are you just playing politics?"

The letter, Ford said, pointed out exactly what mistakes Ford was making.

"When I got this, I was mad as hell, you don't say things like this to the President of the United States," Ford said. "Then I read it again and said, 'I realize he was sending it as a good friend who tells the truth.'"

That good friend to presidents and Army football died in 1989 at the age of ninety-two. Jim Young, then Army's coach, summed up Blaik's achievements: "He will be remembered as one of the greatest coaches of all time and one of the outstanding leaders."

The artificial turf field at Michie Stadium was renamed Blaik Field, to which one of his former players, Joe Cygler, said: "I'm sure he wouldn't like it."

George Welsh

George Welsh played for one of Navy's most accomplished coaches, Eddie Erdelatz. Unlike Erdelatz, Blaik, and most of the other great mentors in Military Academy football history, Welsh went from gridiron sensation to sideline savior.

Not surprisingly, Welsh credits his playing time at Annapolis for shaping him as a naval officer and, later, a Hall of Fame coach for the Midshipmen and at the University of Virginia.

"I think I had certain leadership qualities coming out of high school, but I think the Naval Academy helps you develop them," Welsh said. "I still believe in what they said then about leadership. I learned about what it takes to be a really good leader.

"The first thing they would say was to know your stuff. If you want to be a good naval officer, you've got to know what the hell you're talking about and what you're doing with the ship. That applies to football, too.

"And then they used to say: 'Be a man about it. Stand up for what you believe. If you make a mistake, admit it.'

"If you're the guy in charge, you have got to take responsibility. That applies in football."

The son of an electrician for a coal company in Coaldale, Pennsylvania, Welsh never wanted a career in the mines. He avoided it through football as the best athlete the mining town had ever seen.

A star quarterback who designed plays on his kitchen table using cookies, Welsh learned to prosper under difficult conditions. The school's field was so plagued by soot and rocks that,

Navy coach George Welsh.
Courtesy of the United States Naval Academy

by his senior season, Tigers home games were played in another town.

Yet Coaldale went 18-1-2 with Welsh behind center, and
Welsh showed his academic talents as a class president and

honor student. He also attended Wyoming Seminary Prep and Ivy League schools sought him, but Welsh was entranced by the Army-Navy rivalry and chose Annapolis in 1952.

Welsh started for Navy from 1953–1955, finishing as a runner-up in the 1955 Heisman Trophy balloting won by Howard Cassady of Ohio State. Welsh led the nation in passing and total offense that year.

One sportswriter was so enamored of Welsh's leadership he wrote: "It's uncanny how he manages to come up with the right maneuver practically 100 percent of the time."

That, naturally, would translate to coaching.

But Welsh, a company commander as a Middie, would soon see action aboard ships involved in the Cuban missile crisis and in protecting the Suez Canal.

"One of the things that the Navy did for me was that I got a lot of responsibility at an early age," Welsh says. "I was twenty-three years old and I was on the bridge of a ship. When you're up there, you have a lot of responsibility and whether you like it or not, you get it early. Even though I didn't start coaching until I was thirty, I had that as a background. I had some pretty responsible jobs during my seven years in the Navy."

Welsh had spent a year as an assistant coach at Navy and, after leaving the service in 1963, he sought a full-time coaching position. And found nothing.

Prepared to forget about football, Welsh was considering law school when he received a response from Penn State coach Rip Engle. Welsh was offered a spot on Engle's staff and "jumped at the opportunity, a great start for me in coaching."

In 1973, with Navy in the throes of a slump that saw it go 10-32, Welsh headed back to Annapolis—as head football coach. His first two teams went 4-7.

And then the Coach Welsh years at Navy became as prosperous as the QB Welsh years had been. He went 55-46-1, led the Midshipmen to four straight winning seasons and three bowls before heading to Virginia in 1982.

"When George Welsh took over," recalls Westwood One's Tony Roberts, who has announced more Army-Navy games than anyone, "that is when the tide turned. Heck, there was the 51-0 game, with a 31-point second quarter, the most lopsided game in the history of Army-Navy. It came right out of the blue and Navy turned the thing into a rout.

"It seemed that George had Army's number. He was not only winning, but in routs."

Indeed, the Middies won four straight by an aggregate 138-16.

Such brilliance earned Welsh long looks from other universities, and he eventually was enticed to move to Charlottesville.

At Virginia, which never had gone to a bowl game, Welsh guided the Cavaliers to twelve postseason contests. His career record there was 134-85-3 and he became, along with Bear Bryant, the first coaches to have the best record at two Division 1-A schools.

"You have to pay the price if you're going to be able to win," he said. "You have to think football all the time for eleven months out of the year. If you just think football from August to December, you're going to lose."

George Welsh rarely lost.

18

THE STADIUMS: OF BOWLS AND
VETS AND DUMPS

America's greatest sports rivalry has taken place on the hallowed turf of Yankee Stadium, the Polo Grounds, and the Rose Bowl. At venerable Soldier Field and Franklin Field. At Giants Stadium and PSINet Stadium.

Even at the academies, in Army's historic Michie Stadium and Navy's revered Thompson Stadium.

In all, fifteen venues have hosted Army-Navy. But most of the games have taken place in what many participants and observers have described as "a dump" or "an embarrassment" or even "a travesty."

And that's in reference to not one, but two stadiums that stood only a few football fields away from one another—and that, thankfully, have been laid low by the wrecking ball.

Municipal/JFK Stadium. And Veteran's Stadium (The Vet).

Philadelphia has, by far, been the most common site for Army-Navy games. Franklin Field, on the campus of the

University of Pennsylvania, hosted seventeen of them, beginning in 1899 and ending in 1935. The stadium still stands and Penn still plays its home games there. The famed Penn Relays track meet also is held at Franklin Field which, judging by the millions of comments about Army-Navy football in Philly, was the most satisfactory of the city's venues.

Built in 1895 at a cost of $100,000 for the first Penn Relays, Franklin Field also had the first scoreboard for college football. It is, according to the NCAA, America's oldest stadium still in use for football games, and became the nation's first two-tiered football stadium in 1922.

Two former players who faced off at Franklin Field in the 1904 game won 11-0 by Army were William Halsey, a Navy fullback, and Charlie Thompson, an Army guard. They went on to fame, of course, as Adm. "Bull" Halsey and Maj. Gen. Charles Thompson, and they oversaw the Pacific theater during World War II.

At one of their meetings during the war, Halsey remarked: "General, the last time I saw you, you were rubbing my nose all over Franklin Field." To which Thompson replied: "Admiral, how was I to know you were going to be my boss in the South Pacific?"

In part because Franklin Field was the home of another university, and in greater part because an alternative with 100,000 seats was available, the Army-Navy matchup was moved elsewhere in 1936. The primary home through 1979 was mammoth Municipal Stadium in South Philadelphia, although the 1942 and 1943 games were held at the academies because of security concerns during World War II.

The area in which Municipal Stadium stood now houses four ballparks/arenas: Lincoln Financial Stadium, home of the NFL's Eagles and the current site of Army-Navy meetings; Citizens Bank Park, where baseball's Phillies play; the Wachovia

Center, home of the NBA's 76ers and the NHL's Flyers; and the Wachovia Spectrum. It is one of the most impressive sports complexes in America.

Municipal Stadium, renamed JFK Stadium in 1964, was one of the worst venues in sports history.

Opened in 1926 for the 150th anniversary celebration of the signing of the Declaration of Independence, it also was called Sesqui Stadium and Philadelphia Stadium. By any and all names, it was a dump.

But the 100,000-plus seats in the horseshoe-shaped stadium was attractive, particularly in the heyday of Army-Navy, when tickets were at such a premium that anyone outside the military itself—even those in the government—often had to scramble for entry. Indeed, the first game at Municipal Stadium, a 7-0 Navy win, drew more than 102,000 fans.

Early on, Municipal Stadium, which cost $3 million to build, was a choice destination for top athletes, including heavyweight champion Gene Tunney's 1926 victory over Jack Dempsey, a fight that brought in nearly $2 million in gate receipts, a hefty sum in those days.

But such big events became rare and the stadium was a money loser, even though the Eagles played four seasons there in the early 1930s. The occasional prizefight—Rocky Marciano beat Jersey Joe Walcott there in 1952 in the first title fight offered on closed-circuit television—and concert and religious service did not help the place turn a profit.

Generally, though, Army-Navy was the lone attraction at Municipal Stadium, and most of the fans came from outside Philadelphia, a city considered ideally located between both academies.

"No matter where you play it, the fans are going to show and come early for the pageantry," says Tony Roberts, who has broadcast Army-Navy games on radio for more than three decades. "You never get tired of the march on to the field with the Brigade and the Corps of Cadets.

"You could say some of those games at JFK had character, that place rocked and rolled. I remember many a cold afternoon sitting there doing the game and you ignored the other things because the game was so special.

"One time, with the wind blowing so hard, I remember saying it would be difficult for an airplane to land. And we nearly froze, but it still was a great day for football and a great place because of the character it had."

Of course, Roberts was sitting in the press box all those years. For the fans, things weren't quite so accommodating.

There were few concession stands and, as one frequent attendee said, rarely was there anything worth munching on.

In later years, the capacity of the stadium fell well below 100,000 because many of the bleachers began to rot or completely fall apart. Some years, after another event was held there, the stadium wouldn't even have been cleaned as Army-Navy day approached.

According to the *Washington Post*, the reason the game stayed at the dilapidated stadium was the rent was only $5,000 instead of the usual 15 percent of the gate, which in some years would approach $100,000.

"If you could forget all that negative stuff, it had a personality unlike any stadium I've been in," said Bob Kinney, former Army sports information director. "It was huge, cavernous, with the track around it.

"But it was falling apart at the seams for many of the years we played there. Some wooden benches couldn't be sat on for games, even though the city sold tickets for those rows. People would get squeezed in at the concessions. It was atrocious; everything was in need of repair.

"I remember one year, Navy had played Notre Dame there weeks before and they had not even bothered to clean up the place. We even had to bring our own chairs for the locker rooms."

One year, the academies were billed by the city for press box food, and the amount charged came to the equivalent of each media member eating six hot dogs. Hot dogs that most of the reporters—generally known for eating anything—avoided like a missed deadline.

When the city condemned JFK Stadium in the mid-1980s, the game thankfully had moved across the street to the Vet. JFK was the host of the fund-raising Live-Aid concert, held simultaneously with a sister event in London, in 1985, its final major event.

At least the stadium provided some lasting memories of the great football battles held within, and was not a reminder that the Sesquicentennial for which it was built was a financial flop, losing nearly $5 million as only 10 million of the projected 50 million visitors attended the celebration.

While through the decades, the game has been moved around the Northeast, it always has found it's way back to Philadelphia. It landed in the Vet in 1980, when Navy registered its third straight lopsided win, 33-6.

That was the first Army-Navy encounter on artificial turf. It wouldn't be long before academy officials, coaches, trainers, and players would be longing for natural grass, because the Vet's carpet was considered the worst in America, rife with bubbles and dangerous seams.

In fact, in 1993, the Chicago Bears' Wendell Davis wrecked not one but both knees on one play, essentially ending his NFL career. For years, the NFL Players Association's survey of its members consistently showed the Vet as owning the most dangerous playing surface in football.

Indeed, there remained a pocket of support to hold the game at JFK. Navy's athletic director in 1987, J. O. Coppedge, even suggested moving it away from the artificial turf and 66,000 seats in the Vet and back into the old horseshoe.

"It has natural grass and it has a larger seating capacity," Coppedge said, "but it's not in physical shape."

And it hadn't been for more than a decade.

Besides, some players enjoyed the environment at the Vet.

"The Vet was a great stadium to play in," said Ben Kotwicka, captain of the 1996 Army team that went to the Independence Bowl. "The atmosphere was great, just because of the tradition of the stadium, and the fans were close to the field. It always seemed like Philly was the right place to be, a little bit of tradition. The community was always there with open arms and very supportive of the military. We always felt right at home there and welcomed, and thought it was a good place to play a ballgame."

So the Vet was the rivalry's new home from 1980–2001, with the exceptions of 1983 (Rose Bowl), 1989, 1993, 1997, 2002 (Giants Stadium), and 2000 (PSINet).

And while there were many memorable matchups in those two-plus decades, the quality of the site did not match the standards of the rivalry. The Vet, while not deteriorating to the extent of its neighbor, JFK Stadium, was never exactly a showcase stage. As one pundit said, "Having Army-Navy here is like putting a diamond in a tin setting."

Never was that more clear, sadly, than in 1998, when four cadets and five United States Military Academy Prep School students were injured when a railing between the front row of seats and the sideline collapsed. They fell 15 feet to the turf during the ninety-ninth Army-Navy game.

The railing collapsed after Army's Ty Amey ran for a 70-

yard touchdown and a 31-30 lead with 6:08 remaining in a wild game. When television cameras panned to that section of the stands during a timeout, the railing on which the fans leaned gave way.

Play was suspended for thirty-one minutes while the injured were loaded into ambulances.

"All of a sudden, you see the railing giving way and you wonder, are they jumping off the side of a wall and down to the ground?" Roberts said.

But then you see them pile up and you know it's a really serious situation.

It happened right across from the broadcast booth in the corner of the end zone. And then the ambulance came on the field and the paramedics began to administer to the cadets, that's when you knew you had a possibility of some serious injuries.

It's a lot like a serious injury to a player that stops a broadcast for maybe 8-10 minutes. You see a player has been immobilized, he's put on a cart and transported away. It does place a pall in the stadium and in the broadcast—but you have to get back to what you are there to do. The players have to go back to performing and you have to relay what they are doing.

In the back of your mind, it's just like with the players, it is always there—what happened and why? And you're always hoping to get some information from the hospital to relay to the audience. The audience is left hanging and you never want to speculate what the injuries were.

It wasn't until well after the game that any specifics became available.

The most seriously injured Cadet, Kevin Galligan, broke a bone in his neck. He walked out of the hospital the next day, when an investigation already had begun. Wearing a neck brace, Galligan soon returned to the academy.

"I'll guarantee you we're going to make sure something like this never happens again," West Point spokesman Capt. John Cornelio said.

Added Philadelphia mayor Ed Rendell, who was in the midst of a campaign to arrange funding for new stadiums for the Phillies and Eagles—and Army-Navy:

"Any person of common sense knows that a railing like that is not meant to support twenty people leaning on it. It looks very clear that it was a clean break, which means there was no rusting or decay.

"We need two new stadiums. If we let this lease run to its conclusion, the Vet will be over forty years old, which is obviously just inherently dangerous."

Galligan, who would be given an honorable medical discharge from the Army, was not surprised about what happened.

"You can see before it goes, I'm motioning (on the videotape) for the other guys to get back, because I knew something was going to happen with all those guys bearing down on us," he said.

Nearly five years later, a few months before the series would move to the new Lincoln Financial Field, Galligan was awarded $1.05 million in a lawsuit against the city, the company that installed the railings, and the contractor responsible for crowd control at the Army-Navy game.

"It takes some of the pain away," admitted Galligan, who also suffered a mild brain injury. "I wouldn't say it's worth it. I really did want to serve in the infantry and go to Ranger school."

Galligan's father, Frank, graduated from West Point in 1966

and became an Army Ranger. He died in a military helicopter crash when his son was three years old.

Kevin Galligan overcame his injuries enough to graduate from the academy, too, but he could not complete the Infantry Officer Basic Course because of chronic pain in his neck. He received the medical discharge in October 2000.

"I thought I was going to be able to do everything that I intended on doing," Galligan said.

The Vet hosted its final Army-Navy game in 2001, a 26-17 Army win that was the Cadets' only victory from 1999 through 2004.

Oddly, Navy won the first game played at Municipal Stadium, the Vet, Giants Stadium, and the Linc. It also won the only games played at the Rose Bowl (1983) and PSINet in Baltimore (2000).

Philly remains the rivalry's main home. The most recent five-year contract awarded four games from 2004 through 2008 to Lincoln Financial Field, and one (2007) to Baltimore. Each academy's revenue from the deal exceeds $20 million, proving that even when one of the teams struggles to get victories—recently that has been Army—there still is an enormous cachet attached to Army vs. Navy.

"This process reinforced without a doubt that the Army-Navy matchup remains an extremely desirable event, with the highest level of national respect," Navy Athletic Director Chet Gladchuk said.

Indeed, fifteen cities or regions bid for those five contests.

"The number of bids received from cities across the country demonstrates the importance attached to the Army-Navy game and the support of the service academies," said Naval Academy superintendent Lt. Gen. William J. Lennox Jr. "The game truly belongs to America."

Added Army's athletic director at the time, Rick Greenspan:

"Those two cities, Philadelphia and Baltimore, really stepped forward to elevate the status of the game. We feel strongly that the Army-Navy game remains one of our country's national treasures and both cities have proven the ability to honor the game properly."

Honoring it, that is, with the proper kind of stages, which had been long overdue.

19

EPILOGUE

You felt it before you saw it.

The sound was so deafening that your eardrums seemed about to burst.

The ground shook as well, as four Navy F-14 fighter jets roared overhead, their awesome power reverberating for miles around. . . .

You heard it before you saw it.

While you were still recovering from the shock waves of the jets, an orchestra of chop, chop, chop filled the air.

Then into view came seven menacing-looking Apache helicopter gunships from the Army.

The battle-ready flying machines were less noisy than the jets, but delivered the same message loud and clear: *Don't mess with us!*

The awesome military might of the U.S.A. was on display. . . .

A battlefield? No, a football field.

A sea full of Middies at the 2004 Army-Navy game.
Photo by Ken Rappoport

Army versus Navy.

And what's an Army-Navy game without parachutes and pageantry?

About a dozen parachutists leaped from planes with multi-colored chutes. They floated to the turf of Lincoln Financial Field in Philadelphia to the oohs and aahs of some 68,000 spectators.

One after another they dropped to the ground, then quickly dragged their chutes off the field to make way for those that followed.

Finally, the field was cleared for the last two—one from the Army's Golden Knights and another from the Navy's Leapfrogs. They thrilled and delighted the crowd by both landing directly at midfield.

It was part of the breathtaking aerial display at the 2004 service classic.

Earlier, thousands of Middies and Cadets had put on their own display.

The entire student body from both service academies had marched into the stadium column by column in perfect unison. Then they stood in thirty tight, perfectly formed columns from one end of the football field to the other.

Outside, fans were moving through the entrances at a much slower pace. Since the September 11 terrorist attacks, security has been noticeably rigid at major sports events around America. The Iraq war and a step-up in terrorism have put everyone on alert.

And at the 2004 Army-Navy game, the security was tight, tight, tight.

Bomb-sniffing dogs, metal detector screens, and wand searches kept thousands outside the stadium. Fans waited in long lines, some missing a full quarter of the game. Why?

The president of the United States was on hand, and security had to be stricter than usual. The image of George W. Bush could be seen on the giant scoreboard screens as he walked to midfield for the ceremonial pregame coin toss.

The ceremonial coin that Bush flipped had special relevance to the times: it was sent from the Iraqi city of Fallujah.

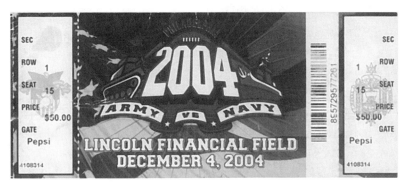

Ticket for the 2004 Army-Navy game.

The American flag is the centerpiece at the 2004 Army-Navy game.
Photo by Ken Rappoport

Even before he had entered Lincoln Financial Field, Bush's presence was announced to the crowd in no uncertain terms. On the way to Philadelphia International Airport, Air Force One roared low over the stadium and dipped a wing in salute to the fans in the upper deck.

Before the game, Bush visited both locker rooms. As he walked into the Navy locker room, the president could not help but see the three jerseys hanging in the doorway in remembrance of former players killed in the service of their country: Ron Winchester and J. P. Blecksmith in Iraq and Scott Zellem in the Pacific.

Winchester was killed in September 2004 by an explosive device while guarding a convoy in western Iraq. Blecksmith was killed by insurgents in Fallujah in October. Zellem died in August when the jet he was flying on a training mission crashed into the Pacific.

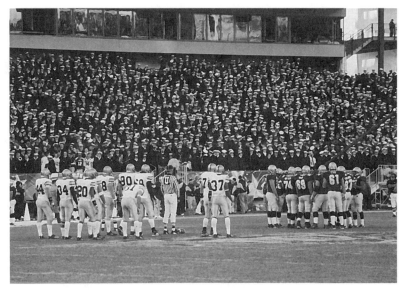

The Midshipmen serve as a backdrop as Navy huddles and Army waits.
Photo by Ken Rappoport

"There are moments, like when we heard that J. P. Blecksmith and Ron Winchester had died and gave the ultimate sacrifice, when it hurts," Navy senior quarterback Aaron Polanco said a week before the game. "But you also see we're blessed to play football now."

The deaths of the players from the Naval Academy hit home with the Army players, as well.

"It's one of those things that touches you when you hear about it," said Army wide receiver Scott Wesley. "You don't know them, but to hear about it is still tough."

The Navy players would place their fallen comrades' jerseys on three chairs at midfield on the sideline during the game. Players from both teams wore patches to honor their fellow servicemen at war.

In the locker room, Bush thanked the Navy players for their

An Army coach goes over game strategy with the players.
Photo by Ken Rappoport

service to the country. He did the same in the Army locker room.

"Listen, good luck today," he told the Cadets. "I know you're going to play hard, but I'm here to tell you thanks for serving your country. I'm proud that you decided to serve the great United States of America. We need your character. We need your class. God bless you all."

Before taking his seat, Bush had been on the field watching warm-ups. Asked who he thought would win, the president replied: "The United States of America."

Meanwhile, long delays continued at the entrances to Lincoln Financial Field for both the fans and the media. The experience of one particular member of the media attested to the unusually demanding security measures deployed:

Making his way to the media entrance, he was stopped by security guards.

Army quarterback Zac Dahman on the run.
Photo by Ken Rappoport

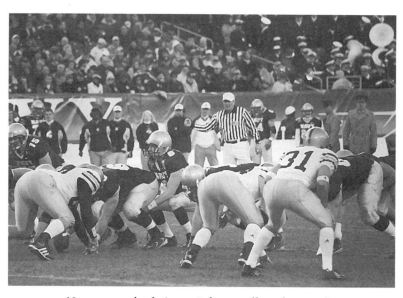

Navy quarterback Aaron Polanco calling the signals.
Photo by Ken Rappoport

The Army cheering section and band.
Photo by Ken Rappoport

"Lay your bag and your camera on the ground and step away!" ordered one of the guards.

As a dog sniffed the bag and camera, the sportswriter was wand-searched up and down his body. Finally given the green light, he was pointed to a door with the sign "Press Room."

He made his way through a maze of underground corridors as he followed signs to the field.

Then, another security check, this time by a secret service man. Finally, the sportswriter was escorted onto the field by another security guard.

The game was well underway by then. The teams were scoreless until Navy started asserting its dominance over a weaker Army opponent in the second period.

At Army-Navy games, it is customary for the president to sit on each side of the field so as not to show favoritism. At half-time, the Cadets and Middies lined up to form a pathway for

President Bush to cross the field from the Army to the Navy side. They stood at attention as the president crossed. Standing a silent vigil were two cadets astride mules, the Army mascot.

Crossing the field, Bush was accompanied by Lt. Gen. William J. Lennox Jr., superintendent of the United States Military Academy. Bush was met by Vice Adm. Rodney P. Rempt, superintendent of the United States Naval Academy. He escorted Bush to the Navy side.

It would be a long day on the football field for Army. Near the end of the game, the Navy goat could be seen eating grass off the field.

It was nothing compared to the way Navy chewed up Army that afternoon.

Following Navy's 42-13 victory that tied the storied series at 49-49-7, another tradition was observed. The players from

Cadets and Middies form a fence as President George W. Bush
changes sides at halftime of the 2004 game.
Photo by Ken Rappoport

*President George W. Bush is shown on the scoreboard screen
as he changes sides.*

Photo by Ken Rappoport

Two cadets astride mules, the Army mascot.

Photo by Ken Rappoport

both sides and the thousands in the stands stood at attention while the alma mater of each school was played by their respective bands.

The game had started at mid-afternoon in bright sunshine. By game's end, the players were standing in the near-dark of a late December afternoon, and a chill had descended on the Linc.

Bitter enemies during the game, they were now the best of friends, part of a higher mission than football. There was total respect for one another, no matter how the game had turned out.

It was a sobering and sentimental moment—many of them would be going off to war, fighting side by side.

Win or lose, they had just finished playing the game of their

During the traditional end to Army-Navy games, the teams listen to the alma mater of each school.
Photo by Ken Rappoport

lives and the moment would be stamped in their memories forever. And in the memories of the fans that watched that day.

"This year three guys (who played for Navy) gave the ultimate sacrifice, gave their lives," Polanco said, referring to Winchester, Blecksmith, and Zellem. "Football is a great thing to do, and we have so much fun. But after our last game, we know there's something bigger we're going into."